SNOW FALLING
ON CEDARS

David Guterson

This edition published by Spark Publishing

Spark Publishing
A Division of SparkNotes LLC
120 Fifth Avenue, 8th Floor
New York, NY 10011

Printed and bound in the United States

ISBN 1-58663-490-9

INTRODUCTION: STOPPING TO BUY SPARKNOTES ON A SNOWY EVENING

Whose words these are you *think* you know.
Your paper's due tomorrow, though;
We're glad to see you stopping here
To get some help before you go.

Lost your course? You'll find it here.
Face tests and essays without fear.
Between the words, good grades at stake:
Get great results throughout the year.

Once school bells caused your heart to quake
As teachers circled each mistake.
Use SparkNotes and no longer weep,
Ace every single test you take.

Yes, books are lovely, dark, and deep,
But only what you grasp you keep,
With hours to go before you sleep,
With hours to go before you sleep.

CONTENTS

CONTEXT

DAVID GUTERSON WAS BORN in Seattle in 1956, and has spent nearly his entire life in Washington, in the area around Puget Sound. After receiving under-graduate and graduate degrees from the University of Washington, he taught high school English on Bainbridge Island near Seattle while writing for *Sports Illustrated* and *Harper's Magazine*. Guterson also published a collection of short stories called *The Country Ahead of Us, The Country Behind* and the nonfiction work *Family Matters: Why Home-schooling Makes Sense*. He and his wife, Robin, have home-schooled all four of their children.

Guterson wrote *Snow Falling on Cedars* over the span of ten years while he was teaching, spending the early morning hours writing. The novel ranks as one of the most popular recent literary nov-els in the United States; it has been a surprise bestseller, with well over one million copies in print. The novel won the PEN / Faulkner Award in 1995, and its success allowed Guterson to quit teaching and write full time. In 1999, the same year a major film adaptation of *Snow Falling on Cedars* opened, Guterson published a second novel, *East of the Mountains,* also set in the Pacific Northwest.

Guterson wrote *Snow Falling on Cedars* based on his personal experiences in the Pacific Northwest and eight years of research. He portrays the fictional community of San Piedro, a culturally and physically isolated island in Puget Sound. The novel concerns the trial of a Japanese-American man accused of killing a white fisher-man and explores the racial tensions that simmer under the surface of the outwardly peaceful, even sleepy, island.

Japanese-Americans, like their fictional counterparts in Guter-son's novel, were often victims of prejudice during World War II. When the Japanese bombed Pearl Harbor in 1941, the United States government ordered the internment of more than 100,000 Japa-nese-Americans, two-thirds of whom were native-born citizens. The government herded these Japanese-Americans into internment camps like prisoners of war, violating their civil rights. Scattered across remote areas of the American West, the camps were places of hardship and very poor living conditions. Additionally, when they were finally released from the camps, many Japanese-Americans, like the Miyamoto family in Guterson's novel, returned home to find that they had lost their jobs, property, savings, and roles in their communities. The United States government did not officially apologize for its actions until nearly fifty years later.

While San Piedro and its characters are fictional, many of the events and circumstances in *Snow Falling on Cedars* are based in reality. In particular, the character of Arthur Chambers, who speaks out against discrimination as the editor of the local newspaper in San Piedro, is based on a real newspaper editor from Bainbridge Island. This editor, Walt Woodward, was one of very few members of the press to oppose publicly the government's internment policies during World War II. Additionally, in an interview with the *New York Times,* Guterson claims to have patterned the character of Nels Gudmundsson—an elderly, morally upright lawyer who defends the accused Japanese man—on his own father.

Though loosely based on real events, *Snow Falling on Cedars* is also heavily influenced by another novel involving a racially charged criminal trial, Harper Lee's *To Kill a Mockingbird,* which was published in 1960. Like Lee, Guterson explores issues of racism using a criminal trial and portrays young people who attempt to come to terms with the forces of fate, love, and hate that have the potential both to divide and unite communities.

PLOT OVERVIEW

O N SAN PIEDRO ISLAND, located off the coast of mainland Washington in the Pacific Northwest, a Japanese-American fisherman named Kabuo Miyamoto goes on trial for the murder of Carl Heine, a well-liked local fisherman and respected war veteran. The date is December 6, 1954, one day before the thirteenth anniversary of the Japanese bombing of Pearl Harbor. Kabuo faces the courtroom silently and with a stiff, upright posture, which the white residents of San Piedro in the courtroom interpret as a sign of Kabuo's cold-blooded remorselessness.

Because San Piedro is a small, isolated island, its residents are extremely careful not to make enemies within their community. Over the years, this caution has cultivated a brooding quiet throughout the island. Carl Heine is an archetypal San Piedro native, silently hoarding his feelings and words as if they were precious nuggets of gold. Carl has returned from World War II with the stony silence of a veteran.

In contrast to Carl, Ishmael Chambers, another war veteran who is about the same age as Carl, makes his living through words. He is the editor of the town newspaper, the San Piedro Review, a position he inherited from his father, Arthur. Yet Ishmael remains silent about one aspect of his personal history, the romantic relationship he once had with a young Japanese-American girl named Hatsue, who is now Kabuo's wife. Ishmael struggles with his memories of this relationship, unable to understand why the beautiful Hatsue, who had been so close to him, abruptly called off the relationship and has treated him with coldness ever since.

Kabuo and his wife believe that it will be impossible for him to receive a fair trial in the postwar anti-Japanese climate. Nonetheless, Kabuo already regards himself as a murderer in a sense. A veteran of World War II himself—having fought for the American side, not the Japanese—he broods over his memories of the enemy soldiers he killed during the war. Kabuo has settled into a quiet acceptance of that guilt, but he has also nurtured an appreciation of his wife and children as marvelous, undeserved gifts.

During the trial, there is little overt expression of racism against Kabuo as a Japanese-American, but it is clear that racism pervades

3

the proceedings. Beneath San Piedro's seeming tranquility and stillness smolders a tension between the island's white residents and its Japanese-American community. During the war, the white residents of San Piedro stood by silently while their Japanese-American neighbors were loaded onto ferries and sent to internment camps. The passive hatred and prejudice common on San Piedro did not originate with the war hysteria, however. Rather, the war merely unleashed and legitimized decades-old prejudices that had previously been suppressed under San Piedro's ethos of silence and avoidance of confrontation.

While Kabuo's trial takes place, the novel repeatedly flashes back in time to episodes that took place years before, interspersing these past events between testimonies and statements given during the trial. During the war, Etta Heine, Carl's rabidly anti-Japanese mother, took advantage of the Miyamoto family's absence to break an agreement her husband made years earlier. Under this agreement, Etta's husband, Carl Heine Sr., had agreed to sell seven acres of his land to Kabuo's father, Zenhichi. The agreement had been informal, since laws at the time forbade Japanese-born residents from purchasing or owning land. Zenhichi made his biannual payments for the land religiously and was just two payments away from full ownership when his family was sent to an internment camp.

The elder Carl died soon after the Miyamotos were sent away. Etta, disgusted with the idea that anyone of Japanese descent would ever own her husband's land, promptly sold the land to a white farmer, Ole Jurgensen, at a higher price than the Miyamotos had paid. When Kabuo returned from the war, he sought to recover the land he felt his family deserved. However, since Ole Jurgensen now owned the land, Kabuo had no choice but to wait patiently until Ole was ready to sell. When Ole finally advertised his farm for sale after suffering a stroke, Kabuo thought that the moment had arrived and rushed to make an offer for the land as soon as he heard that it was available.

Kabuo found that Carl Heine had beaten him to it; Carl had already made arrangements to purchase Ole's land. Hearing Kabuo's pleas, however, Carl agreed to consider selling Kabuo a portion of the land, the small plot that Zenhichi had originally attempted to purchase. Kabuo held out hope that Carl would in fact decide to offer him the land, since he and Carl had been childhood friends. However, Kabuo knew that Carl, though at heart a good man, had struggled with anti-Japanese prejudices ever since the war.

Still undecided about the land sale, Carl went out in his fishing boat on the foggy night of September 15, 1954. His boat ran out of power during the night, leaving him stranded in dense fog in the middle of a shipping channel, a perilous place to be because of the huge freighters that frequently passed through the channel. Fortuitously, Kabuo came upon Carl's boat and helped him. Grateful for Kabuo's kindness, Carl overcame his prejudices and agreed to sell the land to Kabuo.

Unfortunately, Carl died later that night in a freak accident. A large freighter passing through the shipping channel created an enormous wake, a wall of waves high enough to jar Carl's boat violently. Carl, who had been cutting a lantern loose from his mast, was knocked down from the mast and hit his head on the edge of his boat. Knocked unconscious, he fell into the water and drowned.

The authorities began to investigate the case the next day, when Carl's boat was found adrift off the island. The investigation was under the jurisdiction of Art Moran, the local sheriff. The coroner, Horace Whaley, a World War II veteran himself, remarked to the sheriff that Carl's head wound resembled wounds he had seen inflicted by Japanese soldiers skilled in the martial art of kendo. Though Art had at first thought that Carl's death was purely an accident, Horace's comment led him to investigate more closely. The evidence, though circumstantial, seemed to point directly to Kabuo. Not only was Kabuo an expert in kendo, but upon searching Kabuo's boat, Art found a fishing gaff with blood on the handle— blood that, when tested, proved to be of the same relatively rare blood type as Carl's.

There remains no incontrovertible proof of Kabuo's innocence until Ishmael Chambers stumbles across a logbook from a local lighthouse on the evening of the second day of the trial. The logbook, kept by a radioman's assistant who is no longer stationed on San Piedro, records that a large freighter got lost in dense fog off the island on the night of September 15, 1954—the same night Carl died. The radioman, attempting to guide the freighter back on course, advised its crew to steer the huge ship directly through the channel where Carl was fishing that night. According to the logbook, the freighter passed through Carl's area at 1:42 A.M., just five minutes before Carl's waterlogged watch stopped at 1:47 A.M.—the moment Carl plunged, unconscious, into the water. It is clear to Ishmael that the freighter's wake, not Kabuo, is responsible for Carl's death.

The discovery of the report leaves Ishmael tortured with indecision. He knows that as an honest man and especially as a reporter, he is obligated to come forward with any information that bears relevance to the trial. However, Ishmael still struggles with intense bitterness as Hatsue's jilted lover. Ishmael recognizes his intense desire for revenge against Hatsue for breaking his heart.

Ishmael sits on the report through the trial's closing statements. The prosecutor, Alvin Hooks, subtly appeals to the jurors' prejudice in his closing statement, exhorting them to look at Kabuo's stone-faced expression when deciding his guilt. Kabuo's attorney, Nels Gudmundsson, directly addresses the matter of prejudice and urges the jury to decide objectively.

The trial ends, and the jury goes into deliberations. All the jurors adamantly insist on Kabuo's guilt except for one, whose stubbornness prolongs the deliberations and forces them to adjourn for the day. At the last minute, Ishmael reveals the contents of the lighthouse report to Hatsue. The charges against Kabuo are dropped and he is freed from jail, finally reunited with his wife and children.

CHARACTER LIST

Ishmael Chambers The novel's protagonist. Ishmael is the thirty-one-year-old editor of the local paper, the San Piedro Review. He is a World War II veteran, and a gunshot in the war has left him with an amputated left arm. As a young boy, Ishmael had a deep friendship with a local Japanese-American girl, Hatsue Imada. But Hatsue eventually called an abrupt end to the relationship and married Kabuo Miyamoto, leaving Ishmael bitter and resentful.

Hatsue Miyamoto Kabuo's wife, whose maiden name is Hatsue Imada. Hatsue and Ishmael became friends as small children, and by the time they entered their adolescence, Ishmael had fallen in love with her. Hatsue, however, always experienced doubt regarding the nature of her feelings for Ishmael. Throughout her life, Hatsue is torn between her Japanese culture and family background and her desire for a world without societal pressures and prejudices.

Kabuo Miyamoto The Japanese-American fisherman who stands trial for the alleged murder of Carl Heine. When Kabuo was a boy, his family worked as sharecroppers on the strawberry farm owned by Carl Heine, Sr. Like his father, Zenhichi, Kabuo is a master at kendo, the Japanese art of stick fighting. Kabuo considers himself a murderer because he killed enemy soldiers in World War II, in which he fought for the United States Army. Since the war, Kabuo has been consumed with his dream to repurchase his family's land.

Carl Heine The local fisherman who dies mysteriously on the night of September 15, 1954. The son of Etta and Carl Heine Sr., Carl was a high school classmate of Kabuo, Ishmael, and Hatsue's and was particularly good friends with Kabuo. After fighting in World War II, however, Carl struggled with his prejudices toward people of Japanese descent. A physically robust, quiet man, he was greatly respected and admired by residents of San Piedro.

Arthur Chambers Ishmael's father. Arthur founded and edited the San Piedro Review, the most prominent newspaper on the island. Arthur frequently—and courageously— used the editorial column in his newspaper as a forum to condemn the racism directed at San Piedro's Japanese-American residents during World War II. Though his editorials often provoked hostility from much of the community, Arthur maintained a strong heart and firmly believed that his perspective was the correct one.

Helen Chambers Ishmael's mother. Now a widow, Helen remains committed to the principles of tolerance and honesty her husband demonstrated. She doubts that Kabuo's trial is fair. Concerned about Ishmael's solitary and seemingly joyless life, Helen urges her son to get over his emotional issues and fall in love again.

Art Moran The local sheriff. Art initially believes that Carl's death is an accident, but he begins to suspect Kabuo of murder after hearing the coroner's offhand comment that Carl's head wound resembles wounds inflicted by Japanese soldiers skilled in the martial art of kendo. His willingness to make such a leap of logic epitomizes the anti-Japanese sentiment prevalent on San Piedro.

Abel Martinson Art Moran's young and relatively inexperienced deputy.

Horace Whaley The Island County coroner and a World War II veteran. Horace is shattered by his experience as a wartime doctor and feels like a shell of his former self. He envies Carl Heine's strength and vitality even as he examines Carl's corpse.

Judge Llewellyn Fielding The judge presiding over Kabuo's murder trial. Although he lets on to be sleepy and distracted, Judge Fielding is keenly aware of everything that takes place in his courtroom. He understands the racially charged nature of Kabuo's trial and does all he can to diminish the role that racism plays in the proceedings.

Nels Gudmundsson Kabuo's morally upright defense attorney. Nels is in his late seventies, and his health is failing. Though he is blind in one eye, his good eye exudes a sharp, penetrating intelligence.

Alvin Hooks The prosecuting attorney in Kabuo's trial. Hooks charges Kabuo with first-degree murder and is rabidly seeking the death penalty. He subtly appeals to the jury's racism during the trial.

Susan Marie Heine Carl Heine's beautiful, blond widow. When she was seventeen, Susan Marie began to enjoy and relish her sexuality and physical attractiveness, using them to pursue Carl when she was twenty. Though Susan Marie feels that Carl was a hardworking, steady husband and a good lover, she began to worry when she realized that their sex life constituted the core of their marriage.

Carl Heine Sr. Carl Heine's father, who owned the strawberry farm on which the young Kabuo's family lived and worked as sharecroppers.

Etta Heine Carl Heine Sr.'s rabidly racist wife. Etta was furious when her husband agreed to sell seven acres of his strawberry farm to Zenhichi Miyamoto, Kabuo's father. Immediately after her husband's death, Etta sold his land to a white farmer, Ole Jurgensen.

CHARACTER LIST

Ole Jurgensen A farmer and landowner in San Piedro. After Carl Heine Sr. died, Etta sold his strawberry farm to Ole, including the seven acres that Zenhichi Miyamoto had contracted to buy from her husband. When Ole suffers a stroke in June 1954, he puts his farm up for sale, and Carl Heine Jr. quickly snatches it up.

Fujiko Imada Hatsue's mother. While her daughters were growing up, Fujiko was wary of hakujin, the word she used to refer to white Americans. She urged her young daughters to follow their Japanese cultural traditions and roles, and did not want to see them act like white Americans.

Hisao Imada Hatsue's father.

Mrs. Shigemura Hatsue's teacher. When Hatsue was thirteen, her parents sent her to Mrs. Shigemura for training in social graces. Mrs. Shigemura told Hatsue to avoid white men and their bizarre fetishes for Japanese girls and advised Hatsue to marry a good Japanese man. She thus represents the old school of Japanese values.

Zenhichi Miyamoto Kabuo's father. When Kabuo was eight years old, Zenhichi began training him in the Japanese martial art of kendo, or stick fighting, and emphasized the discipline and self-restraint of the art. Like Mrs. Shigemura, Zenhichi embodies traditional Japanese values.

Alexander Van Ness A local boat builder and member of the jury in Kabuo's trial. Van Ness does not believe the evidence proves Kabuo's guilt beyond a reasonable doubt, and he refuses to convict the fisherman of murder until the other jurors effectively convince him of Kabuo's guilt.

ANALYSIS OF MAJOR CHARACTERS

ISHMAEL CHAMBERS

Ishmael Chambers, the protagonist of *Snow Falling on Cedars*, is haunted by the trauma of his past. His rejection by Hatsue Imada and his brief but horrific experience in World War II have left him bitter and resentful. With a broken heart and a missing arm, Ishmael sulks around San Piedro, observing other people's lives but having little personal life of his own. Ishmael reports what he sees in the San Piedro Review, the local newspaper that his father, Arthur, founded.

As a virtual outcast chronicling the lives and events that go on around him, Ishmael plays a role similar to that of the most famous Ishmael of American literature, the narrator of Herman Melville's Moby Dick. Like Melville's narrator, Ishmael Chambers watches as his fellow humans are battered by seemingly impersonal forces: war, prejudice, and the fierce winter storm that blankets San Piedro's cedars in fresh snow. Unlike Melville's Ishmael, however, Ishmael Chambers must learn to accept circumstances that he cannot change, such as Hatsue's rejection of him and the loss of his arm in the war. He must also find the courage and maturity to make choices that influence others' lives. Specifically, Ishmael struggles with the decision about whether to change the course of the trial by sharing evidence from the lighthouse that will exonerate Kabuo.

Ishmael is disillusioned and disappointed because he thinks there is unfairness and injustice in the world. He insists that facts, and facts alone, should decide the fate of individuals. This stubborn idealism is poorly suited to the complexities of human life on San Piedro, a place where the very geography—the confinement of living on a small island—affects the lives and fates of its residents just as much as objective truths. In response to his disillusionment, Ishmael retreats into a cold and antisocial shell. Feeling himself incapable of loving again, he dwells on the legacies of the past, unable to overcome memories of the war and wanting to exact revenge on Hatsue for her rejection. Ishmael's challenge throughout the novel is to emerge from his shell, move forward from his painful past, and become a strong leader as his father was before him.

HATSUE IMADA

More than any other character in the novel, Hatsue is torn between the demands of two seemingly irreconcilable sets of values. The young Ishmael represents one set of values, the belief that individuals have the right to be happy and that they can live in a manner unrestrained by the demands imposed by society. The other set of values, represented most fully by Hatsue's mother, Fujiko, and Mrs. Shigemura, holds that life is inherently full of suffering and misfortune. Individuals must accept the limitations of their time, place, and culture and try their utmost to fulfill their duty to family and community.

Though these two value systems roughly correspond to the cultural division between the whites and the Japanese, Hatsue is proof that such a simplistic division is impossible and that it is inappropriate to assume that all whites feel one way and all Japanese the other. Hatsue feels bound by duty to her parents, but at the same time resents her mother's antiwhite prejudices. As a teenager, she loves Ishmael but feels that their love is somehow wrong. Later, Hatsue learns to accept that she can never love Ishmael and follows her mother's wishes by marrying a Japanese man. Yet when Kabuo informs her of his plans to enlist in the army and fulfill his duty to America, Hatsue tries to make him stay. Her argument is similar to the one Ishmael makes in the cedar tree: two people in love should be together no matter what the rest of society demands from them.

Even after the war, when Kabuo is on trial, Hatsue cannot accept the idea that her husband's fate rests in the hands of an impersonal system of courts and laws. She expects Ishmael to intervene on Kabuo's behalf simply because Ishmael, as the editor of the newspaper, has power and influence that might be used to assist Kabuo's case. Throughout the novel, Hatsue struggles to reconcile the conflicting values of individualistic idealism and stoic passivity. That she never fully achieves this reconciliation suggests that such a struggle never ends.

KABUO MIYAMOTO

Like Carl Heine, Kabuo is a victim of fate. He does not feel that his fate is entirely arbitrary, however. A conscientious and pensive man, Kabuo feels guilty about killing Germans in World War II, even though he was merely doing his duty as a soldier. He had, after all, chosen to serve his country out of a desire to prove his loyalty. Still, Kabuo condemns himself for these wartime killings, believing that the guilt will remain with him even after his death.

Kabuo's feeling of guilt is so pronounced that it haunts him in the same way that Hatsue's rejection and the war haunt Ishmael. Though he is innocent of killing Carl Heine, Kabuo does not feel self-pity about his wrongful imprisonment. Rather, he accepts his trial and potential death sentence as a form of cosmic justice for his earlier murders in the war. However, he has no faith in this system of justice and lies to his attorney because he does not think anyone will believe him. Though Kabuo certainly wants to live, since he loves and appreciates his family, he is not even sure he deserves to be free. In effect, Kabuo puts himself at the mercy of chance because he does not believe in his own right to decide his future.

CARL HEINE

Though he is dead throughout most of *Snow Falling on Cedars*, Carl is a major character in the novel. He embodies both the best and worst aspects of the white community on San Piedro. A physically strong, hardworking, and stoic man, Carl is San Piedro's ideal citizen. He toils for his family's welfare, keeps to himself, and has largely put the trauma of his war experiences behind him. In these respects, Carl is superior to Ishmael, Horace Whaley, Kabuo, and the many other San Piedro residents who are only marginal members of the community.

Though Carl clearly represents many ideals, he also exemplifies the frustrating passivity and closed-mindedness typical of San Piedro's white residents. As we see in his conversations with Kabuo and Susan Marie, Carl has an unthinking and reflexive dislike of people of Japanese origin, even though he and Kabuo used to be close friends as youngsters. Furthermore, Carl is so stoic and emotionally isolated that even his wife feels she does not know him well. Even the other fishermen, ostensibly Carl's closest brethren, feel distant from him.

Carl's importance to the narrative extends beyond his contradictions. When Carl agrees to sell the seven acres of land to Kabuo, he becomes the first of the novel's major characters to find the strength to put the past behind him. It is ironic, therefore, that almost immediately after Carl affirms the power of individual morality, he is killed by the most impersonal of forces: chance.

Themes, Motifs & Symbols

Themes

Themes are the fundamental and often universal ideas explored in a literary work.

The Struggle Between Free Will and Chance

Guterson uses words such as mystery, fate, accident, happenstance, and coincidence to describe the inhuman, uncontrollable, and unknowable forces that govern the universe. Indeed, many events in the world of *Snow Falling on Cedars* simply happen, causelessly and unpredictably. Carl Heine dies because a freighter happens to pass by his boat at the exact time that he is atop his mast, at his most vulnerable. Ishmael happens to survive the storming of Betio while almost everyone else in his platoon dies. The lighthouse radioman, who would have been able to prove that Kabuo was innocent of murdering Carl, happens to be transferred out of San Piedro the morning after Carl's death.

These events, like the motions of the storm and the sea, happen for no reason and without human control. The characters in the novel continuously struggle to exert their own will against such impersonal and random forces. This struggle sometimes entails learning to accept what they cannot change: Ishmael, for instance, must accept that his arm has been lost in the war and that Hatsue does not love him. Sometimes, however, circumstances that appear inevitable and unchangeable—prejudice or war, for example—are the result of human action. Guterson suggests that people can and should act to resist these things. Nels decries prejudice in the courtroom, and Arthur does the same in his newspaper. Kabuo assists Carl in an emergency despite having every reason to disregard him. The challenge facing people, Guterson suggests, is learning to recognize the difference between what is human and therefore changeable and what is inhuman and therefore unchangeable. Drawing on love, compassion, courage, reason, and forgiveness, individuals and societies can and must decide as much of their own fate as they can.

THEMES

THE CYCLICAL NATURE OF PREJUDICE

Snow Falling on Cedars reads like a map of prejudice, clearly show-
ing the fault lines between groups and individuals. Prejudice is pervasive on San Piedro; whites resent and fear the Japanese
immigrants, but reap economic profit from the Japanese-American
residents' discipline and hard work. Envy, mistrust, and greed run
rampant as the island's whites round up, imprison, and exile their
Japanese neighbors when the government gives its internment
order. Yet the Japanese-Americans are not simply victims; in some
ways, they choose to maintain their separateness, partly out of a
sense of superiority. Fujiko, for instance, has contempt for whites
and for American culture in general. Likewise, Kabuo distrusts his
white neighbors so much that he refuses to cooperate with Art
Moran's investigation of Carl's death.

Guterson implies that prejudice runs in such cycles, with each
biased action and attitude reinforcing and generating new prejudice. Characters who are surrounded by such resentments and
biases start to internalize them, allowing them to seep into other
parts of their life. Ishmael, for instance, learns to hate the Japanese
during World War II because he hates Hatsue for having rejected
him. Carl likewise hates the Japanese because the war takes him
from his beloved farm.

Additionally, we see that such prejudices in the novel are not limited to differences in ethnicity. The San Piedro fishermen mistrust
Ishmael because he is an intellectual and makes a living by using
words rather than his hands. Such prejudices remain buried beneath
the surface of the seemingly placid community on the island, but
they have the potential to erupt with violent consequences. The
struggle to identify these prejudices in public and in private is a cen-
tral challenge for the characters of *Snow Falling on Cedars*.

THE LIMITS OF KNOWLEDGE

Ishmael's argument with his mother, Helen, illustrates the limits of
knowledge in the novel. While Ishmael lies and argues that the facts
show Kabuo is guilty, Helen wonders if such facts are ever enough to
justify condemning a man. Ishmael resists his mother's argument
despite his knowledge that the case against Kabuo is dangerously
incomplete and circumstantial.

Guterson suggests that facts and knowledge are not the same
thing. When the young Ishmael tells his father that a newspaper
should report only facts, Arthur responds by asking his son, "Which

facts?" Ishmael ultimately asks the same question when he urges Art Moran to search Carl's boat a second time. As the novel progresses and we learn more about Carl's death, we realize that the facts of the case are never complete. The facts remain important, however, because they are often the only resource we have in making any judgment. As individuals and as a community, the characters in *Snow Falling on Cedars* must use reason when making decisions that could hurt others: weighing Kabuo's guilt or innocence, for example, or sitting idly by as the island's Japanese residents are rounded up and put in prison. In every decision, human beings must rely on facts that are inevitably incomplete. We must accept that our knowledge is limited and must rely on our hearts and our reason to make the right decisions.

MOTIFS

Motifs are recurring structures, contrasts, or literary devices that can help to develop and inform the text's major themes.

THE STORM
The snowstorm beats against the courtroom windows, fells power lines, and sends cars careening into ditches. The storm's fury affects the islanders, interrupting their lives and routines: the jurors are stranded in the courthouse, and fishing comes to a standstill as boats capsize in the harbor. Other incidents of adverse weather likewise affect the course of events. The young Ishmael and Hatsue end up in the cedar tree for the first time because a rainstorm drives them there. The disorienting fog on the water is indirectly responsible for Carl's death because it causes him to lose his way and end up in the risky waters of the shipping channel. Rough seas complicate Ishmael's platoon-landing at Betio during the war, increasing the carnage and losses the platoon suffers. In every case, nature pushes human beings, controls them, and puts them at its mercy. Humans become complacent and seek to survive and cope as best as possible. The storm outside the courtroom is a symbol for the chance, uncontrollable incidents that affect human lives.

THE BODY
Many characters in the novel have bodies that reflect essential qualities of their characters or personalities. For instance, Carl's penis, which Horace notices is twice the size of his own, emphasizes Carl's

former vitality and strength. These qualities won Carl the admiration of San Piedro's islanders, while his sexual drive defined his relationship with his wife. Susan Marie, likewise, has beautiful blond hair, marking her as the physical ideal of the white community on San Piedro. Kabuo's face, which is cold and impassive, conveys treachery and remorselessness to the jurors, while to Kabuo it expresses guilt for World War II bloodshed. Ishmael's amputated arm is a visual token of his incompleteness as a person and his inability to mature into a responsible, active adult. We see that characters in the novel frequently use these physical traits as the basis for judgments about other characters or about themselves—judgments that are often incorrect.

Testimony

Courtroom novels frequently use testimony as the narrative device to tell a story. In *Snow Falling on Cedars,* testimony is the engine that drives the plot. The testimonies of characters who sit on the witness stand inform us of the circumstances of Carl's death and illuminate the stories, biases, and attitudes of various individuals on the island and the community as a whole. Guterson rarely tells us anything in a straightforward narrative voice. Instead, he weaves together a collection of testimonies to create a rich and conflicting portrait of relations on San Piedro.

SYMBOLS

Symbols are objects, characters, figures, or colors used to represent abstract ideas or concepts.

The Cedar Tree

For Ishmael and Hatsue, the cedar tree is a sanctuary from society and the forces of prejudice that attempt to keep them apart. The tree is the only place where they are free to express their love for each another. Hidden in the woods, the cedar tree exists outside of society; dead and hollowed out, it exists outside of time. The tree exists in a different world that is unaffected by chance, circumstance, and the prejudices of others. The tree shelters Ishmael and Hatsue from storms both literal, such as the falling rain and snow, and figurative, such as war and prejudice. The tree's isolation, however, prevents the couple from living fully in the world and from accepting and acknowledging that life is not always fair. For Hatsue, in particular, the tree becomes a prison of deceit, leading her to believe in a relationship that is untenable in the face of the pressures of the outside world. The tree imprisons Ishmael in a similar fashion, locking him into an unrealistic vision of the world that eventually hurts him.

ARTHUR CHAMBERS'S CHAIR

Arthur Chambers's chair, like his study, is empty. The chair represents Arthur's legacy of moral authority and dedication to truth and fairness. Ishmael treats the chair with respect but also with a hint of awkwardness and fear. He does not feel that he fits into the chair, a reflection of his fear that he has not lived up to his father's stature or reputation. When Ishmael finally makes the courageous and mature decision to help Hatsue, the woman who has hurt him, he is able to fill Arthur's chair and draw strength from it.

THE COURTHOUSE

The courthouse embodies humanity's frail but noble attempts to separate right from wrong and guilt from innocence—in effect, to impose order and clarity on an uncaring and chaotic universe. The courthouse is battered by storms and plagued with technical difficulties, such as a faulty radiator and intermittent electric power. The building literally shelters its inhabitants from the storm, but it also symbolically shelters the characters from immoral and irrational acts like discrimination. The courthouse is a highly fragile shelter, however, and is not entirely immune to the storms of chance or human cruelty.

SYMBOLS

ISHMAEL'S CAMERA

Like his father before him, Ishmael carries a camera with him virtually everywhere he goes on San Piedro, recording images from the daily lives of the island's residents. Photographs, like facts, purport to convey an objective and unbiased view of the world. Yet Guterson implies that photographs, like facts, can be easily manipulated to convey a subjective story or perspective. In carrying the camera, Ishmael wields not only the power to tell stories but also the ability to frame people's lives with his own biases.

SUMMARY & ANALYSIS

CHAPTERS 1–3

SUMMARY: CHAPTER 1

The novel opens in a courtroom on San Piedro Island in the Puget Sound region of Washington. The date is December 6, 1954. Kabuo Miyamoto, a Japanese-American fisherman, is on trial for the murder of another local fisherman, a white man named Carl Heine. Kabuo sits in the courtroom, proud and silent, while the court prepares to hear the case. A snowstorm is brewing outside. Inside, jurors, lawyers, reporters, and the public gather for the trial. Among the reporters is Ishmael Chambers, the editor of the local paper and a veteran of World War II. Kabuo's wife, Hatsue, is also in the courtroom. Ishmael had tried to speak with Hatsue before the trial. But Hatsue, for reasons not yet clear, told Ishmael to go away.

SUMMARY: CHAPTER 2

In the courtroom, Alvin Hooks, the prosecuting attorney, questions the local sheriff, Art Moran. Art testifies that Carl Heine's boat, the Susan Marie, was found adrift on the morning of September 16, 1954. Upon boarding the boat and investigating the scene, Art and his deputy, Abel Martinson, found Carl's body trapped in the boat's fishing net underwater. When Art and Abel pulled Carl—a well-built, quiet, and respected fisherman—up into the boat, they discovered an odd wound on his head. The wound later led Art to suspect foul play.

SUMMARY: CHAPTER 3

During cross-examination, Kabuo's defense attorney, Nels Gudmundsson, questions the sheriff about the contents of Carl's boat. Of particular interest is a dead engine battery that was found on the boat. The type of battery is different from the type that Carl normally used to power his boat but it matches the type of battery that Kabuo used on his boat. The elderly Nels, whose failing health has left him frail, raises the possibility that Carl may have fallen out of his boat by accident while he was changing the engine battery.

ANALYSIS: CHAPTERS 1–3

The first chapters of *Snow Falling on Cedars* establish three aspects of the novel's setting. First, Guterson introduces the island itself. The residents of San Piedro live in close proximity to one another and are isolated physically from the rest of the world. Likewise, their antiquated lifestyle of fishing and strawberry-farming separates them culturally from people in Seattle and other nearby urban areas. Together, this physical and cultural isolation heightens the fragility of the community. It also encourages us to think of San Piedro as a microcosm, a smaller world that symbolizes the whole world.

Second, the first few chapters introduce the courtroom. The courtroom is not only the physical setting but also a metaphor for Guterson's overall intent in the novel. While the citizens of San Piedro put Kabuo on trial, Guterson puts the community of San Piedro, and history itself, on trial. Just as a trial relies on testimonies to establish a story, leaving a jury to decide guilt or innocence based on these testimonies, the novel presents testimonies of its characters' beliefs and values, leaving us to decide who is guilty and who is innocent.

Third, Guterson describes the snowstorm brewing outside the courthouse, a storm that lasts through the entire trial. This storm forces the islanders to cooperate, even as they put one of their own members on trial. More important, it represents a force of nature that humans are powerless to control. Yet while a storm rages outside, inside the courtroom people try carefully to determine the guilt or innocence of a man. This tension between the aspects of life that individuals and communities cannot control and those they can and should control persists throughout the novel.

The temporal setting of the trial is also significant, although Guterson does not tell us when the trial is happening until later. The trial takes place over a few days in early December 1954, including December 7. It was on this day in 1941 that Japanese warplanes bombed Pearl Harbor, prompting the United States to enter World War II. Since the trial involves a Japanese-American accused of murdering a white American, this anniversary is charged with significance and heightens tensions in the small, racially mixed community.

Chapter 1 also establishes the novel's three main characters: Ishmael, Hatsue, and Kabuo. Though Guterson includes few details about the characters at this point, our first glimpse provides a lot of information about them. Kabuo is proud and silent, Ishmael is sullen and awkward, and Hatsue is willful and bitter. These brief glimpses of their characters help us better understand each person's motives and perspectives as the novel moves forward.

CHAPTERS 4–6

SUMMARY: CHAPTER 4
Judge Lew Fielding calls a brief recess in the trial. As the courtroom empties, Ishmael moves from the reporters' table to a less conspicuous seat in the gallery, where he reflects on the death of Carl, whom he has known since childhood. Ishmael also muses on his own past: the loss of his arm in World War II, his later stint attending college in Seattle, and his decision to return to San Piedro to follow in the footsteps of his father, Arthur Chambers. Arthur, we learn, founded the *San Piedro Review* after working in the logging business and fighting in World War I. As the editor of the newspaper, Arthur was careful to print only what was true and accurate. Ishmael, though more sullen and cynical than his father, strives to do the same.

The narrative then flashes back to the day following Carl's death. Art Moran is down at the docks, talking with local fishermen about who and what they saw while out on their rounds the previous night. Ishmael approaches the group to ask questions for the story he will print in the newspaper. The fishermen bristle at Ishmael's presence, mistrustful of him because he earns his living with words rather than with his hands. Art is not pleased to see Ishmael either, fearing that he will spread rumors of murder in his newspaper. Ishmael agrees not to characterize Carl's death as a murder on the condition that Art keep him up to date as the investigation goes forward.

SUMMARY: CHAPTER 5
The narrative now moves to the office of the local coroner, Horace Whaley, who is also a practicing physician. Horace was unnerved by the experience of losing soldiers under his care in World War II. Horace considers himself a weakling and a failure, and he envies Carl Heine's strong, well-built body as he examines Carl's corpse. He even notices that Carl's penis is twice the size of his own.

Examining the body, Horace discovers a foamy mixture of air, mucus, and seawater that suggests that Carl died from drowning.

He later notices a deep wound on Carl's head. Horace notes that the wound resembles wounds he saw during the war, on soldiers who had fought in hand-to-hand combat with Japanese soldiers trained in kendo, the art of stick fighting. Horace and Art puzzle over whether the wound was inflicted before or after Carl hit the water.

SUMMARY: CHAPTER 6

The narrative returns to Kabuo's trial. Nels Gudmundsson questions Horace Whaley on the stand. Nels gets the coroner to acknowledge that Carl must have still been breathing when he hit the water, based on the fact that a foamy mix of air, mucus, and seawater had been found in Carl's lungs. Watching the trial, Art Moran remembers the moment he broke the news of Carl's death to Carl's wife, Susan Marie. She had stared mutely, in shock, and then matter-of-factly said she had always known it would happen one day.

ANALYSIS: CHAPTERS 4–6

The narrative in this section builds on the general details of the trial—its participants, its evidence, and the alleged crime for which Kabuo is accused—that Guterson presents in the first three chapters. Much as if we are reading a mystery novel or watching an actual trial, we learn about the alleged crime only through the testimony of various characters. Guterson narrates as if he were seated in the back of the courtroom, listening alongside the other spectators. At certain moments, however, he enters the minds of his characters to show us what they are thinking. For example, Chapter 5 begins with Horace testifying in the courtroom but it quickly switches time and perspective, jumping into Horace's mind as he recollects performing the autopsy on Carl. Guterson continually jumps in time and place in this fashion, moving from the present to the past and from character to character. This narrative tactic ties the past and the present together and helps provide us with a psychological portrait of the entire community.

The portrait of San Piedro that emerges is complex and often ugly. Horace's envy of Carl's penis and the fishermen's wariness toward Ishmael both suggest deep-rooted tension even within San Piedro's white community, in addition to the tension between the whites and the Japanese. Horace, with his damaged nerves, and Ishmael, with his amputated arm, are acutely aware of their inferior status in the community relative to Carl. Horace and Ishmael are passive members of society, whereas Carl, a handsome war hero and hard worker, was an active one, fulfilling the San Piedro ideal. Horace and Ishmael feel marginalized because they are not ideal community members. Yet we learn that the Japanese have an even lower status in the community and are often treated as lesser citizens by its white residents.

Additionally, in this section we begin to see how firmly Ishmael is entrenched in the past. Though Ishmael's look back on his past in Chapter 4 is completely understandable, since it is brought about by his reflection on growing up with Carl Heine, he dwells on his youth more than we might expect. Guterson hints that Ishmael felt compelled to follow in his father's journalistic footsteps and now worries about living up to his father's reputation for integrity and accuracy. Ishmael also dwells on his amputated arm—a defect that, as we begin to see, is a physical counterpart to the emotional void that exists in his life.

CHAPTERS 7–10

SUMMARY: CHAPTER 7

We learn that the Japanese residents of San Piedro first came to the island in the early 1880s, most of them penniless. Many found work in the nearby Port Jefferson lumber mill. After the mill closed, they made a living growing strawberries on their own land or as share-croppers. However, the law forbade noncitizens from owning land and also forbade the naturalization of foreign-born Asian immigrants as United States citizens. Despite these official prejudices, San Piedro made one attempt, annually, to bridge the gap between races. Each summer, a girl of Japanese descent was chosen to be the strawberry princess at the island's Strawberry Festival. Despite the institutional and informal prejudices they faced, the Japanese-American residents of San Piedro were crucial to the local economy as laborers. They carved a niche for themselves in the island's society and prospered—until they were evacuated on March 29, 1942, and sent to internment camps in California and Montana.

Hatsue's mother, Fujiko, had come to America and married Hatsue's father, Hisao Imada, without knowing anything about him. A baishakunin, or professional matchmaker, had arranged the wedding, telling Fujiko that Hisao was a wealthy man. Fujiko felt angry and betrayed when she met Hisao in Seattle and learned he was penniless. Nonetheless, she chose to remain in America, and together she and her husband worked hard at menial jobs, eventually growing to love each other.

In the courtroom, the Japanese-Americans sit together in the back of the gallery, Hatsue among them. She wishes to speak to her husband alone, but the deputy, Abel, forbids her. We learn that Hatsue has started to feel old and now wears makeup. When she was thirteen, her parents sent her to a woman named Mrs. Shigemura for training in manners and social graces. Mrs. Shigemura told her to avoid white men.

We also learn that Hatsue met and married Kabuo while they were in an internment camp. They were married in a small ceremony. On their wedding night, they slept together in one half of her family's room, separated from the others only by a wool blanket and the noise of a radio. There, they had sex for the first time, but with little privacy. Eight days later, Kabuo left to volunteer for the U.S. Army, against Hatsue's wishes.

SUMMARY: CHAPTER 8

The narrative flashes back again, this time to Ishmael's childhood. Ishmael remembers how he and Hatsue played on the beach together as children. When they were ten, they kissed for the first time, holding on to a glass-bottomed box Ishmael often used to look under the surface of the water of the island's tide pools. The kiss was innocent and awkward. Ishmael kissed Hatsue again when they were fourteen. This kiss was more serious; Hatsue stood still and then ran away. They did not speak to each other for ten days, but Ishmael hid in the forest outside Hatsue's house in the evenings, hoping to catch a glimpse of her.

Then, after a day spent harvesting strawberries, Ishmael followed Hatsue to her home. It was raining, but instead of going home she ducked into a hollowed-out cedar tree in the forest. Hatsue had seen Ishmael following her, so she invited him inside to dry out. When Ishmael apologized for kissing her, she replied that she was not sorry. She worried about the controversy their relationship might cause in the community, and then she kissed him. Ishmael felt an overwhelming joy, but also a fear that he might never experience such a moment again.

SUMMARY: CHAPTER 9

Back in the courtroom, Etta Heine, Carl's mother, takes the stand. We learn that Etta was born in Germany and raised on a farm in North Dakota, where she met Carl Heine Sr. and eloped with him to Seattle. The two of them worked at menial jobs in the city before eventually settling on San Piedro.

The narrative flashes back to a scene in 1934 on the Heines' strawberry farm. Carl Heine Sr. agrees to sell seven acres of land to Kabuo's father, Zenhichi Miyamoto. Though Etta is utterly opposed to the transaction, Carl finalizes it in an eight-year lease-to-own contract. Judge Fielding briefly interrupts Etta's flashback, explaining to the jury that such a lease-to-own arrangement was necessary at the time because laws forbade Japanese-born Americans from purchasing or owning land. Returning to 1934, we learn that the American-born Kabuo will turn twenty, the minimum age for legally owning land, in November 1942. Carl Sr., defying Etta's opposition, agrees to turn over ownership of the land to Kabuo upon Zenhichi's final payment.

During Etta's testimony on the stand, she recalls the moment in March 1942 when the Japanese are given only eight days' notice to prepare for their relocation to the internment camps. Zenhichi tells the Heines to take his berries and sell them for whatever they are worth. Otherwise, he says, the berries will go to waste and rot in the fields since the Miyamotos will not be around to harvest them. Carl agrees to harvest the crop on the seven acres in question and take the profit as payment. Etta again objects, making her distrust and dislike for Zenhichi quite clear.

SUMMARY: CHAPTER 10

In the courtroom, Alvin Hooks, the prosecutor, is still questioning Etta. Etta recounts that Carl Sr. died in 1944, at which time she sold the farm to Ole Jurgensen for $1,000 per acre, returning Zenhichi his $4,500 of equity. Etta then moved from her farm to Amity Harbor, the only town on San Piedro, in December 1944. In July 1945, Kabuo called on Etta. Fresh from military service in Italy, Kabuo wanted Etta to allow him to finish paying for the land his father had almost fully purchased. Etta refused, claiming she had not done anything wrong in selling the land to Ole Jurgensen. Kabuo agreed that she didn't do anything illegal but added that she did do something unethical. In response, Etta slammed the door in Kabuo's face.

Etta tells the jury that after this encounter she felt threatened by Kabuo and asked her son, Carl, to keep an eye on him. Alvin Hooks uses this portion of the testimony to argue that a family feud exists between the Heines and the Miyamotos. When Nels cross-examines Etta, he makes the point that in selling her land to Ole instead of to Kabuo, Etta increased her profit by $2,500.

Ole Jurgensen then takes the stand. The old man testifies that, after suffering a stroke in June 1954, he put his farm up for sale in the first week of the following September. Kabuo approached Ole on the day Ole announced the sale, hoping to buy back the seven acres his family had lost. However, Ole had already accepted a down payment for the whole farm from Carl Heine Jr., who had stopped by earlier that day. Carl had told Ole that he wanted to stop fishing and live his dream of farming strawberries instead. Kabuo simply showed up too late to buy the land.

ANALYSIS: CHAPTERS 7–10

This section provides a broader context for the relations we observe between the Japanese-Americans and white Americans on San Piedro. We see that the Japanese have been set apart from the larger San Piedro community both before and after their wartime internment. No law forces people of Japanese descent to sit in the back of the courtroom, for instance, but their unofficial status as second-class citizens makes it socially necessary. Their place at the back of the courtroom reflects their subtle segregation from the community and the delicate nature of their claim to justice.

As Mrs. Shigemura demonstrates, however, the Japanese themselves have a hand in maintaining their separateness. Mrs. Shigemura tells Hatsue to avoid white men, claiming that they treat Japanese girls without respect, as mere exotic objects. We see that from a young age Hatsue has been indoctrinated to distrust the whites as much as the whites distrust the Japanese. The teenage Hatsue's fear that her love affair with Ishmael will cause a controversy is due just as much to her own community's racism as the white community's racism. However, the Japanese community's separation from the broader community gives it greater cohesion. The experience of internment has forced the Japanese-Americans to live together under extreme circumstances. We see the severity of the internment camp's conditions in the fact that despite the extreme respect for privacy and propriety in Japanese culture, Hatsue and

Kabuo must spend their wedding night in the same room as their entire family.

Guterson highlights the hypocrisy of the whites' fear of the Japanese by illustrating that everyone on San Piedro is an immigrant—the only difference is that some have come from Europe while others have come from Asia. Fujiko's life story closely parallels Etta Heine's; both women were born outside the United States, married young, and worked along with their husbands at menial jobs in Seattle before moving to San Piedro. Both Fujiko and Etta learned to resent people different from them—Fujiko indoctrinated her daughter to cling to her Japanese heritage and to distrust whites, while Etta tried to prevent her husband from selling land to Zenhichi simply because he was Japanese. The two women are equally proud and stubborn, equally new to San Piedro, and equally unwilling to tolerate diversity. The similarity ends with the background to their respective distrust. Whereas the Japanese-Americans were forced to live in internment camps during the war, the San Piedro islanders of German ancestry—though also natives of an enemy country—were not the targets of such discrimination.

CHAPTERS 11–14

SUMMARY: CHAPTER 11

> He would have to . . . accept that the mountain of his violent sins was too large to climb in this lifetime.
> (See QUOTATIONS, p. 51)

Kabuo is in his cell during the court recess, staring at the lunch he has not touched. He looks at his reflection in a hand mirror, realizing that he looks cold and hateful. He thinks about all he has missed since he was put in jail: autumn's changing leaves, the squash harvest, and the fall rains. He remembers taking his family to a nearby island for a day of picnicking in August. His mind wanders further into the past, remembering Hatsue as a teenager, picking strawberries on a San Piedro farm.

Kabuo also remembers his argument with Hatsue about his decision to volunteer for the army. Kabuo felt he had to prove something, whereas Hatsue feared he would die or return as a war-hardened monster. Kabuo also recalls his childhood, when at age eight his father began training him in kendo. By the time Kabuo was sixteen, no one on the island could defeat him in kendo. While the older Japanese men still regarded his father as the superior martial artist, they all sensed a warrior's dark ferocity in Kabuo. In light of his war murders, Kabuo now agrees with them. He concludes that the trial is simply one more bit of suffering that he must undergo to pay for the lives he took while fighting for America in World War II.

SUMMARY: CHAPTER 12

When they looked out into the whiteness of the world the wind flung it sharply at their narrowed eyes and foreshortened their view of everything.
(See QUOTATIONS, p. 52)

As the snowstorm grows in ferocity and envelops the island, Ishmael remembers the hollow cedar tree where he and Hatsue often met. In public and at school, they pretended to be only casual acquaintances. Hatsue's emotional reserve often upset Ishmael, but she always justified it by claiming that her parents had trained her to avoid emotional displays. Though she cared about Ishmael, Hatsue was deeply bothered that her relationship with him required her to deceive her parents constantly.

In the fall of 1941, Ishmael and Hatsue began to worry about the war. They were seniors in high school and Hatsue was named the strawberry princess in that year's festival. Though life seemed full, Hatsue and Ishmael were afraid of the future and the changes the war might bring in their lives. From inside the cedar tree, however, the war and its concerns still seemed far away.

SUMMARY: CHAPTER 13

The narrative flashes back to December 1941. The Japanese have just bombed Pearl Harbor. The Imadas and the rest of the Japanese community in San Piedro anxiously crouch around their radios to hear the news. Arthur Chambers publishes a special war edition of the *San Piedro Review,* including information about San Piedro's air-raid safety measures along with an article reporting that San Piedro's Japanese residents have pledged their loyalty to the United States. Arthur points out that while some Japanese Americans' bank accounts have been frozen, no one has even thought to treat the islanders of German descent as possible traitors.

Arthur's supportive stance toward the Japanese-American community earns him threats and angry letters from customers canceling their subscriptions but also letters of support from other people who condemn racism. Arthur publishes all the letters, whether they are supportive or reproachful. Ishmael objects to his father's statements of support for the Japanese, saying the paper should publish only facts, not opinions. Arthur responds, "But which facts? Which facts do we print, Ishmael?"

SUMMARY: CHAPTER 14

The narrative jumps ahead a few months to February 1942. Two FBI agents arrive to search the Imadas' home and confiscate any and all vestiges of the "old country," including a kimono and a bamboo flute. The agents discover a shotgun and some dynamite Hisao uses to clear fields for strawberry planting. According to wartime orders, these items are illegal, so the agents arrest Hisao and take him away.

The government sends Hisao to Montana to dig trenches in a work camp. Fujiko, left with her daughters, tells them the story of how she came to the United States from Japan. She says that she endured hardship and hatred from the *hakujin,* or white people. Now, she predicts, the family will have to endure more hardship.

In the cedar tree with Ishmael, Hatsue worries about their future and tries to be realistic. Ishmael is certain that things will turn out fine, arguing that their love for each other will overcome all obstacles. They kiss, but Hatsue is not convinced. Several weeks later, the U. S. War Relocation Authority orders all Japanese-Americans on the island to prepare for internment. In the cedar tree, Ishmael hatches an elaborate plan to communicate with Hatsue by mail. The two teenagers start to have sex, but Hatsue makes Ishmael stop, crying out in despair. Ishmael asks Hatsue to marry him, but she refuses, saying that she feels that everything about their relationship is wrong. Hatsue runs from the tree, leaving Ishmael for the last time. The next day she and her family depart for the internment camp.

ANALYSIS: CHAPTERS 11–14

This section affords us the first glimpse of the world through Kabuo's eyes. The manner in which Kabuo physically looks at the world reflects his feelings about justice, destiny, and life. As he looks at his reflection in Chapter 11, for example, he sees a hard, blank stare from eyes that "[do] not so much seem to stare right through things as to stare past the present state of the world into a world that was permanently in the distance . . . and at the same time more immediate than the present." Kabuo feels that he does not have control over his present world, so he constantly looks ahead to what he fears will be his future. He fears that his fate has already been decided for him; he realizes that the jury likely interprets his facial expression as haughty and remorseless and will therefore find him guilty. Kabuo accepts his fate, believing that he must pay for the sin of taking lives in the war. He feels that he deserves a guilty verdict even though he is innocent of Carl's death; he believes that murder is murder and that justice is inescapable. Kabuo's posture and stare reflect this stony fatalism and his conviction that his destiny is not in his hands.

Fujiko also has a highly fatalistic worldview. She sees the war and her family's internment as proof that there can never be understanding between the Japanese and the *hakujin*. Fujiko predicts that the war will force her family to become more immersed in Japanese culture, as they will all endure the war's hardships together. When Hatsue protests that not all *hakujin* hate the Japanese, Fujiko counters that *hakujin* are egotistical and therefore fundamentally different from the Japanese. Fujiko believes that living among the *hakujin* will make Hatsue impure. Ironically, it is only the harsh experience of internment that enables Fujiko to keep her daughters isolated from the whites.

Ishmael's beliefs contrast sharply with Kabuo's and Fujiko's. Ishmael insists that his love for Hatsue will triumph over the divisions that arise from their different ethnic backgrounds. He even believes that they will maintain their romance after she is sent to the internment camp. Ishmael holds out this hope because he firmly—and very naïvely—believes that life always makes sense and is always fair. Ishmael's naïveté is further illustrated by his objection to his father's editorial policy. When Ishmael tells his father to print only the facts, he shows his simplistic faith that facts will lead to truth and that truth will lead to justice. The real world is far more complicated than Ishmael is willing to admit. Unlike Fujiko's resentment and Kabuo's fatalism, Ishmael's outlook is based entirely on naïve idealism and the hope that justice, love, and his desire for Hatsue will prevail.

Hatsue's beliefs fall somewhere between those of Ishmael, Kabuo, and Fujiko. Hatsue shares her mother's fears for the future and feels guilty for deceiving her parents about her relationship with Ishmael. Yet when Fujiko tells her that she should avoid *hakujin,* Hatsue disagrees, arguing that people should be judged as individuals rather than stereotyped as members of groups. Hatsue wants to believe that the Japanese and whites can get along because she wants to believe that her love for Ishmael—which feels right when she is in the cedar tree, safe from the realities of the outside world—can exist despite racial differences. Just as the cedar tree cannot shelter her forever, however, Hatsue cannot keep the outside world away. She comes to this realization at the very moment Ishmael tries to have sex with her. Hatsue must make a choice between the two worlds and the two systems of belief. As she pushes Ishmael away, she starts to embrace Fujiko's fatalistic view of the world. As Ishmael tries to enter her, she literally and figuratively shuts him out.

CHAPTERS 15–18

SUMMARY: CHAPTER 15
The following morning, army trucks take San Piedro's Japanese families to the Amity Harbor dock. They embark on the first stage of the long and arduous journey to Manzanar, an internment camp in the deserts of Southern California. At Manzanar, the Japanese-Americans live in cramped barracks that do not adequately protect them from the incessant wind and dust storms. The residents do not speak or complain to each other, however, but merely wander around in a daze like ghosts. Families lose track of one another and children wander off from their parents.

Ishmael's first letter to Hatsue arrives at Manzanar. Ishmael has taken precautions so that the letter will reach Hatsue without her family's knowledge, but this elaborate plan is foiled when Hatsue's sister opens the letter, reads it, and shows it to her mother. Fujiko angrily confronts Hatsue about the letter, ordering her never to write or speak to Ishmael again. Hatsue admits that the relationship was wrong. The following day Hatsue writes Ishmael a letter breaking off their relationship. Within months, Ishmael is a memory, "a persistent ache buried beneath the surface of [Hatsue's] daily life." Hatsue meets Kabuo, and they soon fall in love.

SUMMARY: CHAPTER 16
The narrative leaves Manzanar and rejoins Ishmael, who is now a marine aboard the U. S. S. Heywood, about to storm the island of

Betio, part of the Tarawa Atoll in the South Pacific. Ishmael has been a marine since the late summer of 1942, training first as a rifleman in South Carolina, then as a radio officer in New Zealand. He and his fellow marines load into boats before dawn, then wait for hours in the waters off Betio. When they finally storm the beach, everything goes wrong. Nearly all of Ishmael's company is killed before the men even reach the shore. Ishmael hides behind a seawall for hours, watching soldiers die all around him.

Finally, when evening falls, Ishmael and the remaining troops climb over the seawall to storm the beach. When a bullet hits his left arm, Ishmael drops behind a dead soldier and passes out. He wakes up to find that medics are tending to him. He blacks out again and then wakes up on a ship, surrounded by sick and dying soldiers. Ishmael realizes that his left arm has been amputated. As he recovers in bed, in a morphine-induced stupor, he mutters in confused rage about Hatsue, "that fucking goddamn Jap bitch."

SUMMARY: CHAPTER 17

As the blizzard continues to rage outside the courtroom, the narrative follows several San Piedro islanders as they cope with the storm. Back inside the courtroom, Art Moran testifies that one of the mooring ropes found on Carl Heine's ship did not match the other three ropes but did match those on Kabuo's boat. Furthermore, one of Kabuo's ropes is brand new, indicating that he recently lost one and had to replace it. Art explains that he first thought to search Kabuo's boat after speaking with Etta and Ole about Kabuo's determination to reclaim his father's land.

SUMMARY: CHAPTER 18

The narrative flashes back to the moments just before Kabuo's arrest. Art goes to Judge Fielding's office to request a warrant to search Kabuo's boat. When Art arrives at the dock with the warrant in hand, Kabuo allows the sheriff to search the boat but declares his innocence. Kabuo is eager to get out to sea and start fishing. Art soon discovers the blood-covered gaff, however, and decides to arrest Kabuo on the spot.

ANALYSIS: CHAPTERS 15–18

The internment at Manzanar is paradoxical. While it dehumanizes and confines the Japanese community as a whole, it liberates many of them as individuals, especially the children. As family structures break down under the stress of life in the camp, the children gain a new level of freedom. The Japanese people also feel liberated from the outside world's encroachment on their culture. Hatsue terminates her relationship with Ishmael and brings herself closer to her family. She feels all along that the relationship is wrong and is glad to be completely honest with her mother at last. Meanwhile, meeting Kabuo brings Hatsue closer to her own community. She begins to feel less confusion about her culture and beliefs, identifying more strongly with her Japanese heritage while moving away from her idealism toward fatalism. However, Hatsue does not give in to fatalism entirely; she objects to Kabuo's enlistment in the army and strongly desires that he stay in the camp. Her wish is as idealistic— and perhaps as naïve—as Ishmael's former belief that his love for Hatsue would overcome all obstacles.

Ishmael and Hatsue move in opposite directions after they are separated from each other. Both initially use the cedar tree as an escape from the outside world, a place where they feel safe to love each other and dream about their future. Yet the tree ceases to be a sanctuary for Hatsue and in fact becomes a sort of prison for her as her guilt about deceiving her parents increases. Ironically, when Hatsue enters Manzanar, a real prison, she feels a newfound freedom and security. Ishmael, however, leaves the sanctuary of the cedar tree for the harshest of all storms: the war.

The death and destruction of the war imprison Ishmael emotionally and shatter him physically. He wakes to find his arm amputated and able to think only of Hatsue's rejection of him. Like Hatsue, Ishmael gives up his idealism and his dream of breaking down the barriers between the Japanese and white cultures. Unlike Hatsue, however, he fails to move on to a new identity and is unable to find a new home for himself in his own culture. Unlike Kabuo, who comes to accept that his war experience makes him guilty of murder, Ishmael finds no new belief system or notion of justice. Left with nothing, he lapses into remorse and hatred. As Chapter 16 closes with the image of the wounded Ishmael cursing Hatsue, we see how Ishmael's loss of innocence has left him unable to distinguish between the cruelty of love, which is individual, and the cruelty of war, which is collective.

Guterson narrates Ishmael's battle experience in a straightforward, detached manner, highlighting the absurd cruelty of war. The members of Ishmael's company die so quickly that they do not even have the chance to figure out what is going on around them, let alone be heroes. Military discipline breaks down as the soldiers die in massive numbers. Guterson's descriptions of the sacrifices made by Ishmael and his fellow soldiers suggest the futility of the war as well as the individual's inability to control his fate in such a war.

The chapters that follow Ishmael's battle flashback return us to a world of facts and testimonies. The San Piedro community's attempt to assign guilt and innocence inside the courtroom contrasts sharply with the storm raging outside. As the blizzard sends cars careening into ditches, the islanders are left powerless, able only to hope for their safety. Guterson notes that the island's longest-established residents are highly fatalistic: "[T]hose who had lived on the island a long time knew that the storm's outcome was beyond their control." Out in the storm, the islanders do what little they can to prepare, but they know that they will have to accept whatever the storm brings. Similarly, inside the courtroom, Kabuo has to accept his own fate. Within the confines of the courthouse, however, it is not the forces of nature but a group of people that will deliberate over his fate—just as it is not nature but people who build walls between cultures and wage war. Guterson repeatedly stresses this distinction, challenging us to decide where to draw the line between fate and free will.

CHAPTERS 19–21

SUMMARY: CHAPTER 19

Back in the courtroom, Dr. Sterling Whitman, a hematologist (a blood specialist) from the mainland town of Anacortes, testifies that the blood on Kabuo's fishing gaff is human blood, type B positive. This type matches Carl Heine's and is relatively rare—only ten percent of white males are type B positive. Kabuo, on the other hand, is type O negative, so the blood clearly did not come from him. Though he does not say it explicitly, the prosecutor, Alvin Hooks, clearly implies that the gaff could be the weapon that caused Carl's head wound.

Under cross-examination from Nels Gudmundsson, however, Dr. Sterling admits that he did not find any bone splinters, hair, or skin on the gaff—remnants that one would expect to find if the gaff had been used to inflict Carl's head wound. Dr. Sterling says that it is more likely that the blood came from a minor wound the coroner

found on Carl's hand. In addition, he states that a full twenty percent of the Japanese population has B positive blood, so the blood
on the gaff could have come from any of a number of the island's
Japanese residents.

After the morning recess, Army First Sergeant Victor Maples,
who trained Kabuo's regiment in hand-to-hand combat during the
war, takes the stand. Sergeant Maples testifies that Kabuo demonstrated an incredible expertise at kendo during training, which
impressed the sergeant deeply. In fact, Kabuo was so good at kendo
that Maples asked Kabuo for instruction in the art. Maples tells the
court that he believes Kabuo's kendo skills could be used to kill a
man far larger than himself. Perhaps most damning, Maples
believes that Kabuo was not only capable but also willing to inflict
violence on another man.

SUMMARY: CHAPTER 20

The narrative flashes back to September 9, 1954, about a week
before Carl's death and two days after Kabuo showed up too late to
purchase Ole Jurgensen's land. Carl's wife, Susan Marie, is at home.
Kabuo stops by to talk to Carl about the sale of Ole's land. As Carl
and Kabuo discuss the matter outside, Susan Marie reflects upon
her courtship with Carl. She remembers how she learned to take
pleasure in her sexual attractiveness when she was about seventeen,
and how at twenty she used that allure to pursue Carl.

Carl comes back inside and explains to his wife that Kabuo has
asked to purchase the seven acres of land his father originally tried
to buy. Carl is not sure how to act: he wants to do what is right,
but his dislike for "Japs" makes him reluctant to sell the land.
Also, Carl does not like the way Kabuo reacted when he said he
had to think the matter over; he gets the impression that Kabuo
expected Carl to hand over the land to him immediately. Susan
Marie says nothing more about the matter, believing that it is not
her place to probe her husband's past. When Carl leaves, Susan
Marie thinks about their marriage, and realizes that it is based only
on sexual attraction. She worries about what will happen when
their desire for each other fades.

SUMMARY: CHAPTER 21

The narrative returns to the present, resuming its account of
Kabuo's trial. Susan Marie takes the stand to testify about the
details of Kabuo's visit on September 9. During Nels Gudmunds-

son's cross-examination, she admits that she was not physically present during Carl and Kabuo's conversation about the land. Additionally, Susan Marie concedes that Carl told her he had in fact given Kabuo some reason to hope that the seven acres would be available for purchase. During Susan Marie's testimony, the blizzard raging outside knocks out the electricity in the courtroom.

ANALYSIS : CHAPTERS 19–21

This section provides new depth to the character of Susan Marie Heine. Up to this point, we know little about Susan Marie. Her muted reaction to the news of Carl's death suggests that she has a stoic outlook on life. Similarly, in saying that she always knew that Carl's death would happen like this one day, Susan Marie demonstrates the same kind of passivity in the face of uncontrollable forces that characterizes so many aspects of life on San Piedro. Her relationship with Carl is based only on sexual attraction, so she never fully understands her husband. She does not share the wounds of war and hatred that have plagued Carl, Horace, Ishmael, Kabuo, and others. Susan Marie respects Carl's privacy about his past but also accepts that their relationship must always be limited as a result. Her ability to persevere after losing Carl suggests that such limitations are the compromises that must be made to function in a world governed by chance.

From Susan Marie's testimony we learn that Carl faced a dilemma in deciding whether to sell the land to Kabuo. In his conversation with Susan Marie, Carl admitted his reluctance to sell the land to a "Jap" like Kabuo. Rather than blame his mother for cheating the Miyamotos and then sell the farm to others, Carl tacitly blamed the Japanese for forcing him to abandon his land to fight in the war. In this regard, Carl resembles Ishmael, who blames the Japanese for Hatsue's rejection of him.

The testimonies of Dr. Sterling and Sergeant Maples show how the prosecution attempts to distort the evidence toward a guilty verdict in two ways. Sergeant Maples's testimony is largely insubstantial and circumstantial, as Alvin Hooks attempts to twist the fact of Kabuo's martial-arts skill into a stereotype of Japanese men as violent and murderous. His argument is not factual and attempts to play solely on the jurors' prejudices. The hematologist's testimony, in contrast, *is* based on fact, as the blood type found on the gaff is indeed somewhat uncommon. However, Alvin Hooks fails to mention that fully twenty percent of people of Japanese descent have this blood type. When Nels Gudmundsson makes us aware of this fact in his cross-examination, we realize that Hooks likely omits it on purpose. He has reported the facts only selectively, attempting to hide this bias behind the guise of science. In these testimonies, then, we see that Kabuo faces not only sensationalism and stereotyping, but also insidious attempts to contort even rational arguments in a way that makes him appear guilty.

CHAPTERS 22–24

SUMMARY: CHAPTER 22

People don't have to be unfair, do they?
(See QUOTATIONS, p. 53)

The electricity is still out in the courtroom, so Judge Fielding calls a recess. Ishmael swings by his office to pick up his camera to take pictures of the storm for the paper. Driving carefully along the island's icy roads, he photographs numerous overturned cars and other scenes of the storm's destruction. On one road, he encounters the Imada family; the car Hatsue and Hisao have been riding in has gotten stuck in the snow, leaving them stranded. Ishmael persuades the Imadas to accept a ride home. There is an uncomfortable silence in the car until Hatsue finally breaks it, complaining that Kabuo's trial is unfair. She implies that it is Ishmael's responsibility as a newspaper editor to defend Kabuo in his publication.

SUMMARY: CHAPTER 23

After dropping the Imadas off at their home, Ishmael visits the archives at the coast guard lighthouse to compare the present blizzard to past winter storms. Meanwhile, he thinks back on his first encounter with Hatsue after the war, when he ran into her at the grocery store. Hatsue noticed his arm and expressed regret for his injury. Staring at her newborn baby, Ishmael angrily replied, "The Japs did it." Hatsue treated him coldly after this remark, ignoring his profuse apologies. In a later encounter, Ishmael found Hatsue alone on the beach and begged her to let him hold her one more time. She refused, asking him to leave her alone.

At the lighthouse archives, Ishmael reads over the radio-transmission records for the night of Carl Heine's death. The records show that a large freighter, the S. S. West Corona, radioed for assistance in navigating the thick fog. The radioman on duty at the lighthouse that night advised the Corona to proceed through Ship Channel Bank—the area where Carl was fishing that night—to get back on course. According to the records, the Corona passed through Ship Channel Bank at 1:42 A.M., just five minutes before Carl's watch stopped when he fell overboard. Ishmael realizes that, as a large freighter, the Corona would have produced waves easily large enough to upend Carl's boat and knock him overboard.

Ishmael steals one of the carbon copies of the lighthouse report from that night's log. Then, talking to one of the lighthouse attendants, he learns that Milholland, who was the radioman the night of Carl's death, was transferred off of San Piedro the morning following the incident. With Milholland gone, Ishmael is the only one who could know about the connection between the Corona and Carl's death.

SUMMARY: CHAPTER 24

> "Everything else is ambiguous. Everything else is
> emotions and hunches. At least the facts you can cling
> to; the emotions just float away."
>
> (See QUOTATIONS, p. 54)

Ishmael visits his mother, Helen Chambers, and talks about the case against Kabuo. He lies to his mother, telling her he thinks Kabuo is guilty. Helen, an elegant and educated woman reminiscent of Eleanor Roosevelt, fears that the evidence in the case is circumstantial and incomplete. She wonders if there are ever enough facts to make a conclusive judgment for a punishment as serious as a death sentence. Helen also says that she sees a cold remorselessness in Ishmael, the product of his experience in the war. Since coming back from the war, he has had only shallow, loveless, and infrequent relationships with women—a fact that dismays Helen. She tells him he must get over the psychological wounds of his war years and resume a normal life.

After talking with his mother, Ishmael rereads Hatsue's years-old letter telling him that she does not love him anymore and that she is breaking off the relationship. Ishmael knows that Hatsue realized this loss of love when they began having sex the day before she left for the internment camp. As Hatsue has requested, Ishmael decides to write a newspaper article defending Kabuo, knowing that if he does so, Hatsue will be in his debt.

ANALYSIS : CHAPTERS 22–24

Just as Carl Heine struggled with the decision over whether to bury his grudges and make up for past wrongs, now Ishmael must decide whether to use his power to help Hatsue. Hatsue wants Ishmael to write an editorial about the role racism has played in Kabuo's arrest and trial. Ishmael, however, is reluctant to raise this issue because he still harbors a desire for revenge against Hatsue and the Japanese. When Ishmael finds the lighthouse report that exonerates Kabuo, his dilemma becomes even more urgent. With the trial coming to a close, Ishmael must quickly make the difficult decision of whether to come forward with the evidence. At the end of Chapter 24, when Ishmael decides to write the editorial Hatsue has requested, it initially seems that he has merely reached a decision to comply with her wishes. It proves to be more complicated than that, since Ishmael indicates that his decision to write the editorial is not purely out of concern for Hatsue but also out of a realization that penning the editorial would put Hatsue in his debt. Ishmael struggles to reconcile his simultaneous love and resentment for Hatsue—a struggle that forces Ishmael to choose between desire to get revenge on Hatsue and his desire to live up to his father's legacy of journalistic integrity.

Indeed, the flashbacks of Chapter 23 demonstrate just how strong—and conflicted—Ishmael's feelings for Hatsue are. When Ishmael first sees her after returning from the war, he pointedly expresses his hatred of "the Japs," hinting that she shares part of the blame for his missing arm. In their next encounter, Ishmael suddenly expresses his desire to hold Hatsue one last time. Later, Ishmael lies to his mother about Kabuo's guilt, even after he finds the lighthouse report that clearly exonerates him. Ishmael cannot move on from his wounds from love and war, unable to mediate between his feelings and beliefs. Guterson suggests a subtle parallel between Ishmael's immature unwillingness to move beyond his own disappointments and a larger social immaturity that leads to racism, prejudice, and even war.

CHAPTERS 25–29

SUMMARY : CHAPTER 25
The narrative returns to the courtroom on the third day of Kabuo's trial. Hatsue takes the stand, and Nels Gudmundsson questions her. She is outwardly calm during her testimony, but she struggles to suppress her nervousness. Hatsue tells the court that Kabuo remained optimistic about recovering his family's land after his conversation with Ole Jurgensen, despite the fact that Ole had already accepted a down payment from Carl. Kabuo felt even more optimistic after speaking with Carl. Kabuo came home the morning of September 16 and told Hatsue that he came across Carl stranded in his boat and loaned him a battery. Kabuo said that Carl agreed to sell the seven acres of land to Kabuo for $8,400, leaving Kabuo jubilant.

SUMMARY: CHAPTER 26
Alvin Hooks cross-examines Hatsue on the stand. He gets Hatsue to admit that upon learning of Carl's death, she and Kabuo did not tell anyone about Kabuo's interaction with Carl that night—the incident of the dead battery and Carl's agreement to sell the land—because they feared Kabuo would fall under suspicion and would be accused of Carl's death.

Next on the stand is Josiah Gillanders, the president of the San Piedro Gill-Netters Association. He testifies that gill-netters—fishermen like Carl and Kabuo—board each other's boats only in cases of emergency. Tying two boats together is tricky, Gillanders adds, so it would be virtually impossible to board another man's boat against his will. Despite the fact that minor disputes frequently arise between fishermen, no gill-netter would ever refuse to help another in an emergency. Alvin Hooks offers a hypothetical scenario: Kabuo pretends to have an emergency aboard his boat, asks Carl to tie up next to him and assist him, and then kills Carl with his gaff. Josiah admits that this scenario is indeed more plausible than a forced boarding scenario.

SUMMARY: CHAPTER 27
The narrative flashes back to September, just after Carl's death and Kabuo's arrest. Nels Gudmundsson, who has been assigned to defend Kabuo, visits his client in jail. Kabuo denies that he spoke with Carl Heine the night of Carl's death. Nels does not believe him.

Kabuo admits that he lied because he did not expect to be trusted, citing the smoldering prejudice against Japanese-Americans on San Piedro. Kabuo explains that he was fishing in the impenetrable fog in Ship Channel Bank that night, just as Carl was. Kabuo tells Nels that he answered a distress signal from Carl's boat. One of Carl's batteries had run out of power, so the two fishermen tied their boats together and Kabuo loaned Carl a D-6 battery. Carl's engine used D-8 batteries—a different size—so he used Kabuo's fishing gaff as a hammer to bend the battery hold to accommodate the D-6 battery. Carl cut his hand in the process, leaving blood on the handle of the gaff.

After Kabuo finished assisting Carl, they had a tense conversation—Carl thanked Kabuo for his help and forthrightly admitted that he might not have done the same for Kabuo. Carl then mentioned the land, explaining that his mother sold it while he was off fighting "you goddamned Japs." Kabuo angrily reminded Carl that he was an American citizen, not a Japanese one, and pointed out that Carl's German ancestry never led Kabuo to call him a Nazi. Carl apologized again and offered to sell Kabuo the seven acres of land for $1,200 per acre, the same price Kabuo had agreed to pay Ole Jurgensen for it. Kabuo agreed immediately, and the two fishermen went their separate ways.

SUMMARY: CHAPTER 28

The novel returns to the courtroom, with Kabuo now on the stand. Questioned by Alvin Hooks, Kabuo admits to lying when he was arrested. He acknowledges several details that he had not mentioned before, such as the fact that he replaced the D-6 battery he loaned Carl with a spare from his own shed. Kabuo claims that he was unwilling to cooperate with the police at first out of fear of being judged unfairly. Alvin Hooks emphasizes the inconsistencies in Kabuo's story, saying, "You're a hard man to trust, Mr. Miyamoto."

SUMMARY: CHAPTER 29

> *There are things in this universe that we cannot control, and then there are the things we can.*
>
> (See QUOTATIONS, p. 55)

Alvin Hooks makes his closing arguments to the jury. He urges the jurors to imagine Carl in need of help and at the mercy of Kabuo, who leaps aboard Carl's boat and kills him with the gaff. He implores the jury to look into the face of the accused man to determine his innocence or guilt.

Nels Gudmundsson then offers his closing argument, noting that there is no evidence to suggest Kabuo plotted a murder or had a motive to murder. Nor is there any hard evidence that foul play even occurred. Nels asserts that the trial is not about murder but about prejudice, reminding the jury that Kabuo's face—the face of Japanese America—must not sway their feelings. They must judge him as an individual, an American, and a fellow member of their community.

Closing the trial, Judge Fielding reminds the jury that the charge against Kabuo is first-degree murder. Conviction on this serious charge requires a unanimous ruling by the jury. The judge reminds the jury that it must deliver a guilty verdict only if it is convinced of every element of the charge beyond a reasonable doubt. He reminds the jurors that if they have any reasonable uncertainty regarding the truth of the charges, they are bound by law to find Kabuo not guilty.

ANALYSIS: CHAPTERS 25–29

The testimonies in these chapters alternately address Kabuo's identity within groups and his identity as an individual. This tension between the individual and the community is one of Guterson's constant concerns in the novel, and here we see the different witnesses struggle to define Kabuo in terms of different communities. To Josiah Gillanders, Kabuo's status as a gill-netter overshadows his identity as a Japanese American. When Kabuo assists Carl, it is their shared identity as fishermen that ultimately allows them to put their other differences aside. Carl decides to sell the seven acres to Kabuo because Kabuo has heeded the gill-netters' implicit code of ethics. In their confrontation on the water, Kabuo directly challenges Carl's prejudice and appeals to his reason as an individual. Kabuo also argues that though they are of different races, they are both Americans. They cannot build a relationship if they continue to consider each other "Japs" and *hakujin*. It is only when they encounter each other as fellow fishermen and fellow Americans that they put their prejudices aside.

Prosecutor Alvin Hooks, on the other hand, subtly tries to identify Kabuo as a member of the Japanese community rather than a fisherman. Knowing that the white jurors likely do not regard Japanese-Americans as full members of the San Piedro community, Hooks anticipates and plays on this prejudice in order to build his case against Kabuo. Hooks's hypothetical scenario, in which Kabuo pretends to be in trouble in order to lure Carl Heine to his death, plays on these prejudices, relying on the stereotype of Japanese-Americans as treacherous, poker-faced, cold-blooded killers. Hooks subtly compares Kabuo to the wartime stereotype of the Japanese-American who professes loyalty to the United States while stabbing it in the back. When Hooks tells the jurors to look at Kabuo's face and do their duty as citizens of their community, he implicitly wants them to look at Kabuo's Japanese face—an outsider's face. Hooks wants the jury to find Kabuo guilty because he looks physically different and is therefore not part of their community.

Guterson emphasizes the physical differences between Kabuo and Carl, suggesting that these disparities are what cause the community's opposite perceptions of the two men. Carl embodied San Piedro's ideal citizen: the silent, self-sufficient white fisherman. He was also a war veteran who, unlike the damaged Horace or Ishmael, was able to keep his past safely buried out of sight. The fact that his fellow fishermen hardly knew Carl—and even feared him to some extent—is no longer relevant. In death he is a hero of sorts. Kabuo, by contrast, is the villain but also the victim. A young man born and raised in America who served his country in war even as that same country left his family languishing in an internment camp, Kabuo should be considered a true hero. Yet upon his return to San Piedro he found a community that had no interest in helping him or his fellow Japanese Americans. Kabuo serves as a painful reminder and symbol of the white community's guilt in allowing such discrimination to befall the Japanese-American community. Hooks's plea that the jury do its citizenly duty by once again purging the "Japanese menace" offers the white community retroactive justification for the discrimination it practiced during the war.

Nels Gudmundsson is the only white person to address racism directly in Kabuo's trial; even Ishmael is reluctant to admit that the jury might be biased. This reluctance stems partly from the white community's collective guilt over its treatment of the Japanese. The lack of dialogue about racism also stems from the island community's unwillingness to address conflict among its members. Individual disagreements must be muted in a small town and on a confined island where no one can afford to have too many enemies. Yet when disagreement is muted completely, the community is in danger of committing injustice, even when it operates under the guise of objectivity—as it purports to do during the trial.

CHAPTERS 30–32

SUMMARY : CHAPTER 30

The jurors leave the courtroom to deliberate. Some people file out of the courtroom, while others remain, since the power outage on the island leaves them with nowhere else to stay that is warm and dry. Nels remarks to Ishmael how much he liked and respected his father, Arthur Chambers. Ishmael sees Hatsue on his way out the door, and she again asks Ishmael to defend Kabuo in the San Piedro Review, calling it "[his] father's newspaper." Ishmael points out that he runs the newspaper now and that if Hatsue wishes to talk to him about what he prints in it, she will find him at his mother's house.

Meanwhile, the jurors deliberate. They are unable to reach a verdict that evening because one of the jurors, a local boat builder named Alexander Van Ness, doubts that Kabuo committed premeditated murder. All the other jurors are frustrated, since they strongly believe Kabuo is guilty but are unable to persuade Van Ness to change his mind. With the lone juror preventing the delivery of a verdict, the jury adjourns for the evening.

SUMMARY: CHAPTER 31

Ishmael sits in his father's study that evening, surrounded by the books his father once read. He remembers his father telling him that an enemy on the island was an enemy for life, which makes the islanders careful toward others' feelings but also makes them somewhat brooding and reserved. Ishmael also remembers his father taking him to the Strawberry Festival as a boy. Arthur Chambers told Mr. Fukida, an old Japanese farmer, that he had high hopes for his son. Mr. Fukida replied, "We wish good fortune for him, too. We believe his heart is strong, like his father's. Your son is very good boy."

Ishmael leaves his father's study and goes to his old room, where he rereads the rejection letter from Hatsue. She wrote that because Ishmael had a big heart, she was certain he would do "great things." Ishmael realizes that he has disappointed Hatsue and has failed to live up to her expectations. He gets up, leaves his mother's house, and walks to the cedar tree. Ishmael then decides to go to the Imadas' home and tell them about the records he found at the lighthouse that prove Kabuo's innocence.

SUMMARY: CHAPTER 32

At the Imadas' home, Ishmael shows Hatsue the evidence he has found. Hatsue is grateful and kisses Ishmael on the cheek just before he leaves. She tells him she will always remember his goodness and urges him to leave the past behind and move on with his life.

Early the next morning, Ishmael wakes to his mother telling him that Hatsue is downstairs. Hatsue recalls that Kabuo testified that Carl had tied a lantern to his mast because he had no electricity to power the lights on his boat. Hatsue reasons that if the lantern is still tied to the mast, it proves that Carl's batteries had gone dead. Hatsue and Ishmael take the lighthouse radio transcript to Art Moran, who agrees to look at Carl's boat again.

Art, Abel, and Ishmael visit the boat, which has been kept in sealed storage. Art makes Hatsue stay behind. The men find no lantern on the mast, but do find some cotton twine on the mast that looks as if has been cut with a knife. A smudge of rust on the twine suggests than it had held the lantern's handle. There is also some blood on the mast, and Ishmael reminds Art about the cut that was found on Carl's hand. Ishmael suggests that Carl might have climbed up the mast to cut the lantern loose after Kabuo left; indeed, the coroner found cotton twine and an empty knife sheath in Carl's pockets. Ishmael speculates that the wake of the passing freighter knocked Carl off the mast while he was cutting the lantern loose, which would explain the missing knife and lantern. Finally, the men notice a dent in the boat and find three human hairs lodged there.

After examining the new evidence, Judge Fielding dismisses the charges against Kabuo and sets him free. Kabuo kisses Hatsue as he leaves the courtroom, and Ishmael photographs this kiss for the paper. The narrative flashes back to the moment of Carl's death, as reconstructed by Ishmael. We learn that Carl was in the midst of tying a lantern to the mast when a massive wave from the Corona crashed into his boat, throwing him from the mast. As he fell, his head struck the boat, knocking him unconscious. He fell into the water and drowned.

The novel concludes with a brief scene back in the present. Ishmael is leaning over his typewriter, writing the story of Carl's final moments. He realizes that although the truth of Carl's death has been revealed, the inner truth of Kabuo's heart—or that of Carl's, Hatsue's, or anyone else's, for that matter—will never be known. Ishmael at last understands that "accident rule[s] every corner of the universe except the chambers of the human heart."

ANALYSIS: CHAPTERS 30–32

We see a remarkable transformation in Ishmael in these final chapters, as he is confronted with the choice between doing what is right by saving Kabuo and enacting his revenge against Hatsue by allowing her husband's imprisonment. Damaged and sullen, Ishmael must stop being a mere observer of life and become an active participant. Reaching the decision to come forward with the evidence finally enables him to move on from the past, recovering from the twin wounds of romantic rejection and war. Ishmael also finally abandons his naïveté and idealism, accepting that the world is an imperfect place ruled as much by accident, chance, and fate as it is by choice.

Though Ishmael's decision to step forward and change Kabuo's fate demonstrates that he does have the power of free will, there are other aspects of his life that he cannot change—the war and his rejected love for Hatsue. However, Ishmael finally comes to accept these circumstances as well. His acceptance occurs symbolically when he drives past the harbor and notices boats capsized by the storm. Guterson writes, "It occurred to Ishmael for the first time in his life that such destruction could be beautiful." Ishmael realizes that destruction is part of life—and life, though imperfect, is worth living.

Ishmael's decision to act is a heroic one, since it demonstrates his newfound moral superiority compared to the silence and prejudice of the other islanders. Ishmael's decision also gains symbolic significance because it occurs while he is in his father's study. Sitting in Arthur Chambers's chair, Ishmael finds the strength to fill the place left vacant by his father's death. Ishmael chooses to live up to Mr. Fukida's belief that his "heart is strong" and to fulfill Hatsue's prophecy that he will "do great things." Ironically, this great thing—saving Kabuo—establishes the foundation for a new, healed relationship between Ishmael and Hatsue.

One other man, Alexander Van Ness, also affects Kabuo's fate. Van Ness is a typical San Piedro islander: a local boat builder who works with his hands, not a lawyer or newspaper editor who works with words. Yet the stubborn Van Ness refuses to condemn Kabuo without proof. Van Ness demonstrates that the mainstream white community of San Piedro does have a conscience after all and that one individual's morality can prevent the community from committing yet another injustice.

The new evidence Ishmael presents sends a shockwave through the community, forcing the islanders to accept that Kabuo does not in fact fulfill their worst stereotypes of the Japanese, and that their ideal citizen, Carl Heine, merely died in an accident. This revelation leaves the islanders unable to justify or rationalize Carl's death. There is no discernable reason for Carl's death—it is the result of pure chance, just like the storm that rages over San Piedro during the trial. In the final lines of the novel, Guterson writes that chance rules the universe and suggests that acceptance of this fact is what allows individuals and communities to survive and prosper. Guterson implies that individuals have a choice over their actions. Just as Van Ness stands up for his beliefs, Ishmael puts his selfishness behind him and acts responsibly, and Kabuo and Carl resolve their differences. A community, an island, even an entire world, though buffeted by the storms of chance, can still perform individual acts of love and justice. Though storms that cloak silent cedars in snow are inevitable, the storms of envy, hatred, prejudice, and war are not.

Important Quotations Explained

1. Everything was conjoined by mystery and fate, and in his darkened cell he meditated on this. . . . He would have to . . . accept that the mountain of his violent sins was too large to climb in this lifetime.

In this passage, which concludes Chapter 11, Kabuo confronts his guilt while sitting in his prison cell. He feels intense remorse for killing Germans as a soldier in World War II—a feeling notably absent in, or at least unexpressed by, the novel's white veterans. More than anyone else in the novel, Kabuo accepts that "mystery and fate" dictate the outcome of life. However, he also believes that individuals, "straining and pushing at the shell of identity and distinctness," are responsible for their actions. Kabuo feels that he has sinned by killing Germans, even if he had little or no choice in the matter. Now a prisoner, Kabuo believes he must atone for these sins by accepting punishment, even if this punishment is for a murder he did not commit. The actual reason for the punishment is irrelevant, because Kabuo feels his punishment is deserved. The only freedom he believes he will ever truly experience, therefore, is the freedom to accept his guilt.

QUOTATIONS

2.   When they looked out into the whiteness of the world
     the wind flung it sharply at their narrowed eyes and
     foreshortened their view of everything.

This passage, near the beginning of Chapter 12, illustrates Guterson's use of the snowstorm as a motif in the novel. Relentless and impersonal, the storm repeatedly batters the island, leaving the islanders at its mercy. Guterson implies that the storm is like the universe: cold and impersonal, the product of random chance that humans are powerless to control. Relentlessly pummeling the courthouse, the storm symbolically lashes at humanity's frail attempts to sort out right from wrong and guilt from innocence within the courtroom. Those who go outside and face the storm directly lose their sense of direction and vision and are thrust into a nearly primitive struggle to survive. Everything else—such as abstract concepts like justice and love—is obliterated. In "foreshorten[ing] their view of everything," the storm forces people to look into the "whiteness of the world." This last phrase is likely a reference to Herman Melville's famous chapter in *Moby Dick*—titled "The Whiteness of the Whale"—in which the narrator equates the "all-consuming" whiteness of the whale with chaos, disorder, and the powerlessness of the individual to influence his or her fate.

3. "I'm talking about people . . . who can do things
    because they run newspapers or arrest people or
    convict them or decide about their lives. People don't
    have to be unfair, do they?"

Hatsue confronts Ishmael with these words near the end of Chapter 22. She urges him to write something in the *San Piedro Review* to defend Kabuo and expose the racist nature of the trial. Ishmael's reply—that Hatsue, or anyone else for that matter, should not expect fairness—stems from his resentment of Hatsue and is a veiled reference to her rejection of him. Hatsue seeks to empower Ishmael with her response here. She may still feel some guilt over rejecting Ishmael, but she insists that people do have the power to intervene against chance. Specifically, Hatsue means that Ishmael has the power to affect the future if he chooses to be brave, kind, and mature enough. Ishmael knows that Hatsue is right but has no response to her pleas. At this moment, we realize that the novel's main conflict is Ishmael's struggle to overcome his cynicism and disillusionment and help the woman who caused his resentment. He must accept that life is not always fair or just but that there are aspects of life that need not be left to chance.

4. "Everything else is ambiguous. Everything else is
    emotions and hunches. At least the facts you can cling
    to; the emotions just float away."

Midway through Chapter 24, Ishmael and his mother, Helen Chambers, debate Kabuo's guilt. Ishmael pretends to think that Kabuo is guilty, despite having just discovered crucial evidence at the lighthouse that effectively exonerates Kabuo. Moreover, after his conversation with Hatsue, Ishmael knows that although "[e]verything else is ambiguous," he has a responsibility to do what he can to ensure that justice prevails. In his conversation with his mother, Ishmael stubbornly clings to certain convictions that he knows are untrue. He believes that only facts matter and that facts are always clear and objective. Ishmael's mother, however, realizes that her son's convictions are merely a shell behind which he hides. She implies that one emotion in particular—love—is stronger than fact and reason. Through Helen's debate with her son, Guterson explores how humans can live together in a universe governed by chance. Helen offers a compelling answer: human beings cannot ever really know the facts or the truth, but they can choose to love one another. Later, after Ishmael decides to overcome his resentment and chooses to help Kabuo, he grasps his mother's sentiment, understanding that chance has the power to rule everything in the world except the heart.

5. "There are things in this universe that we cannot control, and there are the things we can. . . . Let fate, coincidence, and accident conspire; human beings must act on reason."

During his closing arguments in Chapter 29, Nels Gudmundsson offers this interpretation of the task before the jury. Nels offers a different sort of argument from that of Helen Chambers. Whereas Helen questions whether facts can lead to truth and instead believes in love, Nels emphasizes the ability—and duty—of people to think and act rationally. He wants the jury to realize that it has the power to control events and that it should not leave them to chance. In offering these contrasting viewpoints from Helen and Nels, Guterson suggests that if love is one way to survive the storms of fate, reason is another. Though love is fragile and reason is imperfect, Nels and Helen argue that these human forces can be strong and can affect the outcomes of events. With this message from Nels to the jury, Guterson emphasizes the challenge of doing everything in our power to rise above chance and circumstance.

KEY FACTS

FULL TITLE
Snow Falling on Cedars

AUTHOR
David Guterson

TYPE OF WORK
Novel

GENRE
Courtroom drama; historical novel; coming-of-age novel

LANGUAGE
English

TIME AND PLACE WRITTEN
United States, 1984–1994

DATE OF FIRST PUBLICATION
1994

PUBLISHER
Harcourt Brace and Company

NARRATOR
An anonymous third-person narrator

POINT OF VIEW
The narrator speaks in the third person and is omniscient, able to see all of the action, both past and present, and aware of what is going on inside the minds of all the characters. The narrator alternates between a straightforward narrative of events and moments of subjective narration from within the minds of various characters.

TONE
The narrator's tone is serious and distant, though at times sympathetic to the characters.

TENSE

Past, with flashbacks between the trial (December 1954) and various earlier events and interactions

SETTING (TIME)

December 1954, with flashbacks

SETTING (PLACE)

San Piedro, a fictional island in Puget Sound, Washington; flashbacks include scenes in Seattle, Montana, California, Japan, the Tarawa Atoll in the South Pacific, and other places

PROTAGONIST

Ishmael Chambers

MAJOR CONFLICT

Kabuo Miyamoto stands trial for the murder of Carl Heine, while Ishmael Chambers struggles to overcome his emotionally and physically shattered past.

RISING ACTION

Kabuo's arrest for murder; Hatsue's request for Ishmael's help; Ishmael's bitterness about Hatsue's rejection of him

CLIMAX

Ishmael's discovery, in Chapter 23, of evidence proving Kabuo's innocence brings Ishmael's conflicting desires to hurt and help Hatsue to a breaking point.

FALLING ACTION

Ishmael's rereading of Hatsue's letter as he sits in his father's study; Ishmael's decision to help Hatsue by coming forward with the evidence that exonerates Kabuo; Judge Fielding's dismissal of the charges against Kabuo

THEMES

The struggle between free will and chance; the cyclical nature of prejudice; the limits of knowledge

MOTIFS

The storm; the body; testimony

SYMBOLS

The cedar tree; Arthur Chambers's chair; the courthouse; Ishmael's camera

KEY FACTS

FORESHADOWING

The snowstorm brewing outside the courthouse at the beginning of the trial hints at the impersonal forces, such as prejudice, that will be at work during the trial. Arthur Chambers's question to Ishmael about which facts the newspaper should print hints at the unreliability of people's perceptions of the truth.

KEY FACTS

STUDY QUESTIONS & ESSAY TOPICS

STUDY QUESTIONS

1. *How does Guterson use Kabuo's criminal trial to explore prejudice against Japanese-Americans?*

Kabuo's trial illustrates both the legal and social aspects of discrimination. The American legal system is supposed to ensure the fair, objective judgment of an accused individual's guilt or innocence. However, the laws of this system can themselves institutionalize racial prejudice. As Judge Fielding explains, Japanese immigrants were legally barred from owning land prior to World War II. This racist law prevented Carl Heine Sr. from selling his land to Zenhichi Miyamoto, which in turn led to the dispute between Kabuo and Carl. Additionally, it was an executive order—not itself a law but an order carrying the force of law—that sent Japanese-Americans to internment camps and forced them to relinquish the few possessions they did own. The legacy of discrimination in the law has contributed to Kabuo's predicament, as well as to the predicaments of many Japanese-Americans in the years after the war.

　In addition to highlighting the legal aspects of anti-Japanese prejudice, Kabuo's trial shows how prejudice can taint the pursuit of objective truth and justice. Full of racist stereotypes of the Japanese, the white community has already presumed Kabuo guilty before the first witness even testifies. The prosecutor, Alvin Hooks, manipulates the jury's prejudice to try to bring about Kabuo's conviction. In his final statement, he asks the jury to look at Kabuo's face and decide whether he is guilty. In doing so, Hooks subtly prods the jury to use their biases to judge whether this Japanese-American individual is guilty of a crime. Hooks effectively puts Kabuo—and all Japanese-Americans—on trial for the events of World War II. The coincidence that the second day of Kabuo's trial is December 7, 1954, the thirteenth anniversary of Japan's surprise bombing of Pearl Harbor, further weighs against him, despite the fact that these events have no bearing on whether he killed Carl Heine. Finally, the courtroom itself reflects the persistent racism in society; while the whites sit in front and participate in the trial, the Japanese-Americans sit in the back and, fearing harassment, remain silent. Taken as a whole, the criminal trial demonstrates the disparity between the ideals and reality of America's legal system and society.

2.   *Guterson alternates between scenes taking place in the courtroom in the present and flashbacks from the past. What effect does such a narrative structure have?*

In alternating between court testimony and flashbacks, Guterson parallels the legal system's case against Kabuo in the literal courtroom with the Japanese-American community's case against their white government and neighbors in the courtroom of memory. Balancing these two different trials, the narrative illustrates the influence of the past on the present. During Etta Heine's testimony against Kabuo, for instance, we learn that Kabuo was angry with Etta for selling the land that he felt belonged to his family. Before Etta finishes testifying, however, a flashback to a time before the war shows us that Etta has always resented the Japanese and that she used the Japanese internment as a pretext for cheating the Miyamotos out of their land. The prejudiced nature of the laws and the prejudiced atmosphere at Kabuo's trial prevent us from learning the whole story. The flashbacks, however, fill in the gaps in the story and illustrate the biases that bear on the trial. As we see with Etta, the behavior of whites toward Japanese before, during, and after World War II is often legal but immoral. In this sense, the flashbacks allow us to see a fuller picture of the past and present, where the morality—not simply the legality—of individual and collective behavior is on trial.

3. *How does Alvin Hooks use the jurors' prejudices against Japanese-Americans in an effort to win his case against Kabuo?*

At one point during the trial, Hooks offers a hypothetical scenario in which Kabuo pretends to be in trouble at sea to lure Carl to his death. Hooks's scenario plays to the white jurors' stereotype of Japanese-Americans as remorseless traitors and murderers. Hooks subtly casts Kabuo in the light of the pervasive wartime belief that Japanese-Americans professed false loyalty to the United States. During his closing arguments, Hooks again tries to appeal to the jurors' prejudices by telling them to look at Kabuo's face and do their duty as citizens of their community. Hooks uses logic in his closing arguments that closely parallels the logic of wartime hysteria. He invites the people of San Piedro to be good citizens by again purging the "Japanese menace" from their community. Hooks reinforces the white community's racism by reawakening the same prejudices that allowed San Piedro's whites to accept passively—and in many cases even profit from—the Japanese internment. In giving their racism some legitimacy, Hooks offers the whites of San Piedro a justification for their behavior during the war, insisting that their fears of Japanese treachery and murder are valid.

SUGGESTED ESSAY TOPICS

1. What dramatic purpose does the snowstorm serve? How does Guterson relate the storm to his narrative?

2. Does Ishmael's decision to bring the lighthouse evidence to Judge Fielding's attention represent a major development in Ishmael's character? What is the significance of Ishmael's decision?

3. The novel presents several different codes of behavior, each associated with a different character. What are some of these codes and how do they differ?

4. Considering the demographics of San Piedro's population, what is ironic about the prejudice against Japanese immigrants and their descendants? How does Guterson develop this irony?

5. Why is Sergeant Maples an inappropriate expert witness on kendo?

QUESTIONS & ESSAYS

Review & Resources

Quiz

1. What is the significance of the date of the second day of Kabuo's trial?

   A. It is the first day of the strawberry harvest
   B. It is the anniversary of the bombing of Pearl Harbor
   C. It is Kabuo and Hatsue's wedding anniversary
   D. It is traditionally the stormiest day of the year

2. Who is Alvin Hooks?

   A. The prosecuting attorney
   B. The sheriff
   C. The sheriff's deputy
   D. The coroner

3. Why does the sheriff suspect that Carl Heine was murdered?

   A. Carl had called on the radio to report that he was being attacked
   B. Carl's body was in several pieces
   C. Carl's blood was all over the boat
   D. Carl had a strange-looking wound on his head

4. What is Ishmael's job?

   A. Fisherman
   B. Photographer
   C. Investigator
   D. Newspaper editor

5. What does Mrs. Shigemura tell Hatsue?

    A. That she should return to Japan

    B. That the *hakujin* deserved to be bombed by
the Japanese

    C. That she should avoid white men

    D. That she should marry Kabuo Miyamoto

6. What does Kabuo do immediately after marrying Hatsue?

    A. He kills four Germans

    B. He volunteers for the U. S. Army

    C. He returns to San Piedro to claim his father's land

    D. He confronts Ishmael about Ishmael's love for Hatsue

7. Why does Hatsue run away from Ishmael when he kisses her at age fourteen?

    A. She is afraid their relationship will cause a scandal

    B. She does not love Ishmael

    C. She wants to make love with him in the cedar tree

    D. She is late for her job picking strawberries on the
Nitta family farm

8. To which of the following do Carl Heine Sr. and Zenhichi Miyamoto agree?

    A. Carl senior will sell seven acres of land to Zenhichi

    B. Zenhichi will farm Carl senior's land in return for
teaching kendo to Carl junior

    C. Carl senior will lease seven acres of land to Zenhichi
for eight years, then sell it to Kabuo

    D. Carl senior will hold onto Zenhichi's money while the
Miyamotos are interned at Manzanar

9. Why is Zenhichi unable to buy the land from Carl senior outright?

    A. Carl does not want to sell to a "Jap"

    B. Etta will not let Carl sell the land

    C. Zenhichi is too old

    D. The law prevents noncitizens from owning land

10. Why does Etta Heine sell the seven acres of farmland to Ole Jurgensen instead of to the Miyamotos?

    A. She can make more money that way

    B. She dislikes Japanese people

    C. Both of the above

    D. Neither of the above

11. What happens to Kabuo when he is eight years old?

    A. He kisses Hatsue

    B. His father teaches him how to farm strawberries

    C. His father teaches him the art of kendo

    D. He gets into a fight with Carl Heine

12. What does Arthur Chambers print in the *San Piedro Review* after the bombing of Pearl Harbor?

    A. A notice that San Piedro's residents of Japanese descent have pledged their loyalty to the United States

    B. A prediction that San Piedro will fall victim to a second attack by the Japanese

    C. His belief that San Piedro's citizens of German descent ought to be treated with equal suspicion

    D. All of the above

13. Why do the FBI agents arrest Hisao Imada?

    A. He refuses to let them search his property without a warrant

    B. They find dynamite and a shotgun on his property

    C. They have orders to arrest whomever they wish

    D. None of the above

14. What does Fujiko Imada predict?

    A. That Hatsue will marry Kabuo

    B. That Hatsue will suffer for having deceived her mother

    C. That the Japanese will beat the Americans in the war

    D. That the Japanese will suffer more hardship at the hands of white people

15. What do Hatsue and Ishmael do together in their last meeting at the cedar tree?

    A.   They kiss

    B.   They start to have sex

    C.   They talk about getting married

    D.   All of the above

16. What does Fujiko do when she discovers Ishmael's love letter to Hatsue?

    A.   She sends Ishmael a letter telling him never to contact Hatsue again

    B.   She confronts Hatsue and makes her promise to end the relationship

    C.   She hides the letter so Hatsue will never be able to read it

    D.   She tries to convince Hatsue that Kabuo would be a better husband than Ishmael

17. Why does Art Moran decide to arrest Kabuo?

    A.   He discovers a fishing gaff in Kabuo's boat with blood on the handle

    B.   He is suspicious that Kabuo has something to hide

    C.   He notices that Kabuo's boat has a new battery

    D.   He overhears news that Etta Heine felt threatened by Kabuo

18. Which of the following does Susan Marie Heine believe regarding her relationship to Carl?

    A.   That they will have nothing to talk about if Carl stops fishing and becomes a farmer

    B.   That Carl will cheat on her

    C.   That Carl expects her to raise his children without help from him

    D.   That their relationship will fall apart when their sexual desire for each other fades

19. What happens during Susan Marie's testimony?

    A. The power in the courtroom goes out
    B. She starts crying and is unable to continue testifying
    C. Ishmael interrupts the trial to show the evidence he has discovered in the lighthouse
    D. Judge Fielding explains to the jury that Washington law forbade the Japanese from owning land

20. What does Hatsue urge Ishmael to do when he drives her home?

    A. Get over their love affair
    B. Investigate for clues that might prove that Kabuo is innocent
    C. Use his position as editor of the newspaper to defend Kabuo publicly
    D. Put snow tires on his car

21. What does Ishmael discover when he takes a trip to the lighthouse?

    A. Records indicating that a large freighter passed through the waters where Carl was fishing at the time he died
    B. Records indicating that no one was manning the lighthouse on the night of Carl's death
    C. That a coast guard radioman heard Carl radioing for help on the night of his death
    D. That there is a coast guard radioman who could exonerate Kabuo but who is not willing to testify at the trial

22. What does Ishmael decide while rereading the rejection letter Hatsue sends him?

    A. That he never really loved Hatsue anyway
    B. That he must get revenge for Hatsue's rejection at any cost
    C. That he can never fall in love again
    D. That he will write an article in the paper defending Kabuo

23. Who is Josiah Gillanders?

    A. A blood specialist from Anacortes
    B. President of the San Piedro Gill-Netters Association
    C. A coast guard radioman
    D. A local farmer

24. What does Carl do when Kabuo lends him a battery?

    A. He admits that he might not have done the same for Kabuo
    B. He calls Kabuo a "Jap"
    C. He offers to sell seven acres of his land to Kabuo
    D. All of the above

25. Why does the jury not immediately find Kabuo guilty?

    A. The jurors are completely unable to agree with one another
    B. The jurors are swayed by Ishmael's editorial about the trial
    C. One of the jurors refuses to convict Kabuo without sleeping on the decision first
    D. Judge Fielding tells the jurors to wait while he gathers some new evidence

ANSWER KEY:
1: B; 2: A; 3: D; 4: D; 5: C; 6: B; 7: A; 8: C; 9: D; 10: C; 11: C; 12: A; 13: B; 14: D; 15: D; 16: B; 17: A; 18: D; 19: A; 20: C; 21: A; 22: D; 23: B; 24: D; 25: C

Suggestions for Further Reading

HOGAN, KATHY. *Cohassett Beach Chronicles: World War II in the Pacific Northwest.* Corvallis, Oregon: Oregon State University Press, 1995.

HOUSTON, JEANNE WAKATSUKI. *Farewell to Manzanar: A True Story of Japanese American Experience During and After the World War II Internment.* New York: Bantam, 1973.

LASKIN, DAVID. *Rains All the Time: A Connoisseur's History of Weather in the Pacific Northwest.* Seattle, Washington: Sasquatch Books, 1997.

MURRAY, ALICE YANG, ED. *What Did the Internment of Japanese Americans Mean?* Boston: Bedford / St. Martin's Press, 2000.

SCHWANTES, CARLOS, ED. *Pacific Northwest in World War II.* Manhattan, Kansas: Sunflower University Press, 1986.

UNITED STATES COMMISSION ON WARTIME RELOCATION AND INTERNMENT OF CIVILIANS. *Personal Justice Denied: Report of the Commission on Wartime Relocation and Internment of Civilians.* Washington, D.C.: Civil Liberties Public Education Fund and Seattle, Washington: University of Washington Press, 1997.

REVIEW & RESOURCES

A Note on the Type

The typeface used in SparkNotes study guides is Sabon, created by master typographer Jan Tschichold in 1964. Tschichold revolutionized the field of graphic design twice: first with his use of asymmetrical layouts and sanserif type in the 1930s when he was affiliated with the Bauhaus, then by abandoning assymetry and calling for a return to the classic ideals of design. Sabon, his only extant typeface, is emblematic of his latter program: Tschichold's design is a recreation of the types made by Claude Garamond, the great French typographer of the Renaissance, and his contemporary Robert Granjon. Fittingly, it is named for Garamond's apprentice, Jacques Sabon.

SparkNotes
Test Preparation
Guides

The SparkNotes team figured it was time to cut standardized tests down to size. We've studied the tests for you, so that SparkNotes test prep guides are:

Smarter:
Packed with critical-thinking skills and test-
taking strategies that will improve your score.

Better:
Fully up to date, covering all new features of the tests,
with study tips on every type of question.

Faster:
Our books cover exactly what you need to
know for the test. No more, no less.

SparkNotes Study Guides: